Isaias Powers

Quiet Places with Jesus

40 Guided Imagery Meditations for Personal Prayer

TWENTY-THIRD PUBLICATIONS
Mystic, Connecticut

Twelfth printing 1991

Twenty-Third Publications
185 Willow Street
P.O. Box 180
Mystic, CT 06355
(203) 536-2611

ISBN 0-89622-086-9
Library of Congress Catalog Card Number 78-64452

Contents

Some Preliminary Remarks

Most people want to pray. There is a sense of rightness within each of us that feels even more "right" when we take the time, as Jesus did, to "go away to a quiet place" in order to praise God in secret, to thank Him for His goodness, to ask for help and to get advice or warning or encouragement for the time ahead.

There are many methods of prayer. They range all the way from simple aspirations to the most elaborately detailed discipline that takes a lifetime to learn. All methods serve their purpose if they permit the person to be present to the possibilities of God's grace.

For prayer to be "successful" (that is, for grace to have "worked") does not depend on an emotional "high," or even on the awareness that "I really prayed well." The only criterion is that which was proclaimed by Christ:

"By their fruits you will know them."
(Matthew 7:15-20; 12:33)

If the time spent in prayer endows the person with more kindness, patience, hope, joy, gratitude, love, serenity, faith, thoughtfulness, gentleness, courage, humility, wisdom, compassion, a sense of oneness and purpose with all humanity . . . then God's grace is most certainly at work.

Anyhow, *we* don't pray. The Holy Spirit within us does the praying.

Various methods of prayer are simply what they claim to be— no more—simply methods. All that humans can do is "get the soil ready," "get the static out of the air," prepare an atmosphere of relaxed alertness, wait for the Lord to work. The Holy Spirit, within us, prays to God our Father; the Holy Spirit, in our name, receives the things we need—insights to understand, determination to improve, stamina to endure. This book of forty meditations suggests the method of *guided imagery*. It is a good way to pray, especially for those who have busy schedules or harried nerves or easily distracted psyches. Like all forms of Christian prayer, it relies on faith and accepts as primary the power of the living Word of God as revealed in Sacred Scripture.

"Guided Imagery Meditation" differs from other methods in its approach to memory and imagination. It takes seriously their power to influence thought patterns. Guided Imagery does not suggest that a person suddenly put the brakes on and try to grind down to a halt after a busy day. Too many people are just not able to do this. As a result, instead of meditating, they are left floundering. For many people, memory and imagination can too easily move them away from that attitude of serene alertness which is so necessary for prayer to be what it is meant to be.*

In a sense, this book deals with "spiritual ecology." Hyperactive memory and anxious imagination frequently distract the mind. They are the "bugs" that pollute the atmosphere of recollection. Using these meditations as a kind of "debugging aerosol," we can quiet down long enough for the Holy Spirit to do the work He wants to do—and will do—as long as we permit His presence . . . and His possibilities.

---

*See Appendix for a more detailed explanation of the power that memory and imagination have to help, or harm, our prayer.

Guidelines for Using this Manual of Meditations

The 40 meditations in this book are a series of "Do-It-Yourself Exercises." They suggest ideas that may help put your mind at rest so that your heart can turn to God.

They are simply *nudges* to get your memory and imagination working in productive ways—helping you instead of distracting you. In no way are they intended to put any *demands* on you. If you should begin to worry, "Am I doing it right?"—this would be another burden of anxiety; and anxiety is the thing that needs to be avoided.

A different setting has been suggested for each day. This was done so that the meditations would not become repetitive, and so that each "quiet place" would somehow fit the Gospel message. Some you will find more appropriate than others; this is to be expected. It may be that some of the settings will trigger painful associations for you. To think of a "small island off the seacoast," for example, might upset a person who almost drowned in such a setting. If the image recalls such an unpleasant memory, think up a different one for yourself. There is a wide variety of them in this book.

If you find one particular setting very helpful, stay with it. There will be a few that you will find very meaningful. There will be circumstances, in both the Gospel message and the Guided Imagery, which resonate clearly to your own experiences . . . and in which Christ speaks to you personally and profoundly. Stay with this, too. Mark the particular meditations that were "made just for you." Return to these often; God was making special note of them as well. He, doubtless, has much more to say on the subject.

Frequently you will find a series of four dots coming after certain phrases in the meditations. It is the only punctuation that can emphasize the purpose of "lagging time." The dots are stage directions. They indicate: "Slow down. . . ." "Put the book on your lap. . . ." "Stay with your thoughts until they are finished. . . ." "Give Jesus a chance to respond; and continue to be alert to this response as long as it seems right to you. . . ."

Sometimes it will seem as though the half-hour went by so quickly, you will want to stay longer with the gentle urgency of God. Do so, if you can afford the time. Other days will seem dull, as if nothing happened at all. There can be many reasons for this— poor health that day; bad sleep the night before; extraordinary demands for energy have exhausted you; that particular Gospel message, or my suggestions, have little interest. Do not be disturbed by this reaction. Such unevenness of feeling is predictable in a series of meditations that continues for 40 days. Even so, it is still recommended that you make the attempt, even on "dry days," for at least 20 minutes. Sometimes God has a way of reaching people, in the most fortuitous ways, with the most unlikely material.

One final comment. I want to explain how I wrote this book. It was just before Lent in 1976 when I decided to write down a series of Guided Imagery Meditations. The decision came at the best time of the year. This is the season—more than any other—when people take prayer seriously. There are 40 Gospel readings between Ash Wednesday and the Easter Vigil of Holy Saturday. They are a pocket-sized compendium of all that Jesus said and did. They also accurately convey the pace of events as portrayed by the Catholic Church from Apostolic times—the teachings, the healings, the formation of disciples, the gathering storm of enmity, the final incidents and the instructions of Holy Week.

Early each morning, I read the Gospel of that day. I ruminated on these passages personally—trying to discover what they meant to me. Somehow (only God knows how) a certain phrase, a certain part of the day's Gospel, would stand out. It seemed to be calling for my attention, directing my thoughts in a particular way.

The first part of each day's meditation is the *Gospel Reflection*, as it occurred to me. It is by no means meant to be a full explanation of that part of scripture, or even a homily or "pious thought for the day." It is simply my own reflection on the Word of God, which set up the prayer that followed.

The second part of each day's meditation is the prayer itself. With the Gospel in mind, I sat down in chapel, or in another quiet place, and let my mind and heart become alert to the ways in which the Holy Spirit might be communicating His message to me.

Certain images suggested themselves. Some were based on time-honored images used by storytellers and psychotherapists. Others came, willy-nilly, out of my own head. They served me because they helped to put memory and imagination at my disposal—to keep me centered in the present time—to be aware of God's possibilities with me.

They have helped me. Perhaps they will help you, too. It is all God's work, whatever happens.

May Blessed Mary, the greatest example of prayer—and St. Luke, the foremost evangelist of our Lord's insistence on prayer—guide you to a place of peace, a hold on hope, a capacity for unclutteredness . . . and to such a habit of constant prayer that you will no longer need any manuals or methods . . . when God will speak plainly—without parables—to your heart.

1
Jesus and Quiet Prayer

*Jesus said, "Be on guard against performing religious
acts for people to see. Otherwise expect no recompense
from your heavenly Father . . . Whenever you pray, go
to your room, close your door, and pray to your Father
in private. . ."*

Matt. 6:1-18

Reflection:

"Secrets," often enough, have deafening ways of screaming out.
This is true not only in the obvious situation of a gossip's tattletal-
ing; it is also true, at times, when a person is alone, enveloped in
solitude, not moving a muscle of his larynx.

When a person closes the door from others and goes to a secret
place—composing himself for prayer or for taking stock of himself—that person is not necessarily closed off from the market-
place or neighborhood or schoolyard or office or family table.
"People" (in the sense of the images of the people) can still mo-
nopolize thoughts, even in solitude. In such cases, being alone is
not all that "secret." Quiet time gets to be quite noisy with remembered litanies of past put-downs and regretted let-downs:

"I tried so hard to win somebody's approval, or to earn
respect, or to get them to realize how well I was putting
up with my sickness or the hard times I was going
through—and they weren't impressed!"

Disillusionment takes over then, or self-pity, or anger (or all
three!). Our secret time of reflection gives way to the memory of
clucking tongues or remembered disapprovals or frowning faces.
When this happens, we are no better than the Pharisees of today's

Gospel, who performed their good works only to be seen by others. They did good "for the sake of show." We need to pray—to *really* pray in secret—in order to do good simply because good is good to do.

Meditation:

In your imagination,
go to a lovely meadow. . . .
There is a tree beside the meadow
and a little chapel over on the other side. . . .
Jesus gently lets you be aware of His presence.
He waves and slowly walks toward you.
Give Him time;
take all the time you need to welcome Him
and to let Him be beside you. . . .

When you are ready, tell Him about your disillusionment
(that whole area of "others not appreciating me. . . .")

Jesus, knowing what He said in the Gospel,
looks kindly and patiently at you
and leads you to the chapel behind the tree.
You are with Him like an invited eavesdropper
as He prays for you to the Father. . . .

After His prayer, He turns to you
and gently tells you
how you, too, can pray to God in secret. . . .
how to avoid discouragement
when others are not impressed by you. . . .
and how to do good simply because it is good to do. . . .

2
Jesus on Self-Denial

Jesus said to all: "Whoever wishes to be my follower must deny his very self . . . Whoever would save his life will lose it, and whoever loses his life for my sake will save it."
                                                        Luke 9:22-25

Reflection:

You already know how you've learned Christ's lesson in today's Gospel. On the physical and psychological levels, you've obeyed the basic principle of growth: "We must die in order to live; we must put to death what we *are* in order to enter the life of what we can *become*."

When you were born, you had no choice. Instinct obeyed Christ's teaching of "death to life" the first time. Life in your mother's womb was safe—no troubles at all. Then the umbilical cord was cut—you "died" to the life of security to feel the pain of heat and cold and noise. Yet, with it all, you are glad it happened; death to the embryonic life ushered in new life, more complex and less confining.

After a year or so, you took your first baby steps. You had to die to "crawling through life," risking the balancing act on just two legs and a possible nosebleed if you fell. Even so, the "dying," again, gave you new possibilities of life—new worlds opened up to you because you were free to walk on your own.

The same principle applied when you died to pre-kindergarten life and entered school. It was hard and scary to give up the security of being "king" or "queen" in a home you had grown accustomed to; you had to become just one of many children competing for attention. Now, in hindsight, you're glad you went to school—it opened up new areas of growth.

Leaving grammar school, "dying" to that life in order to enter high-school life, followed the same procedure. And on and on . . .

Spiritual growth follows a similar lesson plan. Granted, it is risky; it always is to die to what one is secure in. But we must. We must detach ourselves from whatever we cling to. We must die to possessiveness in order to let God draw us further into the ways of living He has planned for us.

Whenever we do this, we are entering Mary's kind of prayer — not hanging on to what we have; rather we "let *it be done* to us."

Meditation:

Using your imagination,
go to a favorite room that's in your memory. . . .
Be comfortable.
Let Jesus knock on the door.
He and four good friends of yours,
who knew you at different stages of your life
bring in a camera and screen. . . .

All six of you prepare things for a private showing:
Jesus plays "re-runs" of your life, from the very beginning.
As the movie rolls along,
He comments on the way you kept bursting out
of a small, secure, comfortable kind of life
into a different way of living
that was, with all its sorrows and added burdens,
fuller and more complex. . . .

Let our Lord thank you — in His own way —
for the courage you have already shown. . . .

Let your four friends add their good memories of you
as well. . . .

Finally, ask Jesus for some hints
about the patterns for growth that are still in store for you.
Remain in silence —
let Jesus reply if He wants to,
as He wants to. . . .

3
Jesus on Indignations

John (the Baptist's) disciples came to Jesus with the objection, "Why is it that while we and the Pharisees fast, your disciples do not?" Jesus said to them: "How can wedding guests go in mourning as long as the groom is with them? When ... the groom is taken away, then they will fast."

Matt. 9:14-15

Reflection:

You know how it is to be bothered by the actions of somebody else. It might be a long-standing enemy, or a group you never liked; it might be a person whom you used to like, but who now "bugs" you. You question their actions with irritation in your voice:

"Why is he doing that to his family?"
"Why is she so irresponsible?"
"How do those people get away with it?"

There are people whose happiness (or happy-go-luckyness) you and I resent. We are suspicious of the way they go through life.

This puzzlement—this gnawing indignation—seems to be behind the statement made by the disciples of John the Baptist. "How do they (the Apostles) get away with not fasting like the rest of us?"

Jesus drained off the anger of their mood as a doctor drains off the poison of a snake bite. He changed the subject: "They are with Me now, and so it is time for cheerfulness. They celebrate My presence as friends do at a wedding party. Fasting is for remembering their personal hopelessness. Their time for doing this will come. But not now."

Jesus reminded the disciples of John that the Apostles had a destiny different from theirs. Perhaps the spirit of today's Gospel can help us heal our envy of enemies and our irritation with those who seem so sure of themselves when we think they have no good reason to be so.

Meditation:

In your imagination,
take yourself to a football stadium. . . .
You are in the bleachers, far away from the field,
sitting beside a stranger. . . .

It is not a football game you are watching;
you are watching the present life-situation of a person
(or group)
who stirs up your indignation or envy. . . .

As you watch, revive your personal reasons
for wondering, "What's with them (him/her)?"
"Why do they act that way?"
Much as irate fans sound off from their bleacher seats,
ventilate all your negative feelings
about the bad behavior and suspected motives
of those you are criticizing so vehemently. . . .

Then let the scene subside;
the crowds go home.
You are the only one remaining—
you and the stranger beside you.
You now recognize the stranger as Jesus. . . .

You are a bit embarrassed to realize He has heard your tirade.
Yet, you stand your ground
(for your indignation is not without righteousness!).

Let Him speak to you as He spoke to the disciples of John. . . .

Perhaps He will suggest that they have a different destiny
—a different blend of *celebration and sorrow*—
than yours. . . .

Let Jesus gently ask you to give Him the responsibility
of judging those people who seem to "bug" you so. . . .

It may be, also,
that Our Lord has some remarks to make
about when fasting will follow the feasts of *your* destiny. . . .
and in what ways feasting will follow your fasts. . . .

4
Jesus on Burdens
We Don't Need

*Jesus said . . . "The healthy do not need a doctor; sick
people do. I have not come to invite the self-righteous
to a change of heart, but sinners."*

Luke 5:27-32

Reflection:

Jesus talks about two classes of people today:

A.) Those He *can* reach with His words and healing powers because they sense their need.
B.) Those He *cannot* reach, because they have concentrated on their own self-righteousness and on their superiority over others.

Jesus is able to reach the "Class A" people. He is powerless to help the other class.

You know, from your own experience, how impossible it is to communicate with a chronic griper, a "chip on the shoulder" individual, one who restlessly complains, "Isn't it awful nowadays . . . Isn't it awful about the kids, the parents, the schools, the church, the world . . ."

It's an old truism: "You can lead a horse to water, but you can't make him drink." The truism is not true for horses. You can work the horse all day and make him sweat. Then you can lead him to the water's edge and lower down the harness . . . and he will drink. His body tells him of his need.

The truism, untrue for horses, is true for humans: You can bring a person to the source of healing; but unless he recognizes his need for healing, he will not accept it. And he will not recognize his need if he thinks the problem is somebody else's—"Nothing wrong with me—it's the others who need to change their ways!"

There is a bit of the "class B" person in us all—every one of us. At times we, too, abort Christ's chances to heal and help us. We are not ready to be healed; we are grumbling about other people, so sensitive to their faults that we forget our own. We need prayer to remind us . . .

Meditation:

In your imagination,
go to a room that is uncomfortable to you.
You are alone,
sitting in a straight-backed chair,
facing the wall. . . .

Let the burdens and imperfections of other people
(all their irritating and sinful ways)
lie heavy on your shoulders. . . .
Feel the weight of these burdens for a while—
be uncomfortable. . . .
Let words flash on the wall, like a neon sign,
saying, "Isn't it awful. . . ."

Then let Jesus knock on the door.
Invite Him in
but don't turn around yet. . . .

Feel the presence of Jesus
as He enters your burden-laden room . . .
Let Him put His hand on your shoulder.
Sit down together in comfortable chairs
beside a warm fireplace . . .

Perhaps our Lord will speak to you:
"Let me gently relieve you of these burdens.
Give them to Me.
I know what to do with them. You don't.

"Now cheer up a little bit.
Come and relax in an easy chair.
I'll share a simple meal with you;
and we can talk—just you and I."

Tell Jesus, in your own words,
about the wounds you still have hurting inside you. . . .

Welcome His healing power. . . .
and let Him give you good advice,
good "preventive medicine,"
for the times ahead. . . .

5
Jesus—Good News About Judgment

Jesus said, "The king will say to those on his right hand, 'Come, you have my Father's blessing!... For I was hungry and you gave me food, thirsty and you gave me drink, a stranger and you welcomed me, naked and you clothed me, ill and you comforted me, in prison and you came to visit me.'"

Matt. 25:31-46

Reflection:

Judgment is usually frightening to think about. It's a moment of dread—we will be errant school-children put "on the carpet" in the principal's office, certain of being expelled from school; or else we will be imperfect football players dreading the Monday afternoon's replay of Saturday's game, certain the coach is going to spend the whole time reprimanding us for our mistakes.

Yet it is Jesus who will be our judge at Judgment Day—the same Jesus who so gently drew people to Him by love and patient forgiveness. It will not be an "either/or situation"—"one mistake in your lives and you go to Hell!"

Judgment will be measured on a scale: 60% kindness in your life contrasted to 40% meanness ... or maybe 70%/30% ... or maybe 20%/80%. Each one of us will be judged according to our deeds, according to our care for other people: friends, family, fellow workers ... whomever we associate with, day by day.

It is not too helpful to meditate on the mean side of our character. Assume, for the moment, that you are a "60% good person," caring and trying to help those who are hungry, or thirsty for approval, or shy (feeling like a stranger), or nakedly sensitive to faultfinders, or sick (physically or mentally), or caged ("in prison") by some hurt or some compulsion. Assume that you have done so 60% of the time, with motives that were partly selfish (40%) and partly unselfish (60%).

Because success builds on success, and because memory of past goodness can be a carrier of confidence for further efforts, it would be well to spend some time reflecting on the possibility that God will judge us favorably, pleased with our caring ways.

Meditation:

In your imagination,
go to the entrance of a king's palace. . . .
Feel somewhat embarrassed
as you are greeted by the servant
who ushers you in to the magnificently furnished formal room. . . .

The servant offers you a glass of wine,
invites you to relax,
and places a large full-length mirror
(a magic mirror) beside you . . .

Quietly—without fanfare of any kind—
people come into the room.
They are people
whom you have helped somehow.
(Take as much time as you please
to welcome them into your consciousness again. . . .)

They show you, in the mirror,
how unhappy they were before you helped them—
hungry or thirsty or naked to faultfinders,
or shy,
or wasting away in some psychological prison
of their own compulsions—

In the mirror, you see them as they *once were;*
in person, you see them as they *became,*
after the kindness (whatever it was) that you gave them.
(One at a time, they express their gratitude to you,
in their own way. . . .)

Then let Jesus come through the mirror.
(For the magic mirror was Jesus all the time. . . .)
Let Him speak to you,
with words that He chooses that you hear,
about today's Gospel. . . .

And let Him remind you of other caring tasks—
other hungry, thirsty, sick, imprisoned people—
whom He wants you to be more aware of
with your helping ways. . . .

6
Jesus on Discouragement

Jesus said, "Your Father knows what you need. This is how you are to pray: 'Our Father in heaven . . . your kingdom come. . . .' "

Matt. 6:7-15

Reflection:

Christ's teaching on prayer really deserves a book of its own, a whole series of meditations.

The six phrases in the "Our Father" are really clues pointing out six basic attitudes that we must develop. St. Matthew writes in "shorthand" here. All four Gospels present Christ's fuller teaching that is summed up in this one prayer.

Jesus did not say, "When you pray, say these *words*." He said, "When you pray, this is *how* you do it!" or, "Pray *this way*—have these attitudes in your mind and heart when you become aware of your relationship with God, your Father."

The second clue has been most important to me—"Father, Thy Kingdom come!" To the degree that I mean what I say when I pray this phrase, I do not get discouraged by other people's disapproval. I often do get discouraged. (Most probably, you do too.) I get "down" when people criticize me, or write me off their list, or show that I haven't lived up to their expectations somehow.

When I let myself get discouraged by such disapproval, I effectively put myself "into *their* kingdom" and give them the power to judge me as "not okay."

But nobody has that power—I don't have it myself. When I remember this, I am not so easily upset. I need quiet prayer (most likely, you do too) so that I won't forget to remember.

Meditation:

In your imagination,
take yourself to the Olympic Games in some far-off city. . . .

Imagine yourself competing in the diving competition.
You try and try to dive well
—you *are* diving well—
but the judges keep giving you a bad score,
preferring others to you. . . .
You are sad and discouraged. . . .

Now let your memory shift from diving
to some situations of your real life in the recent past:
times when you were saddened and discouraged
because somebody (or some others)
judged you as not acceptable,
or not living up to their expectations,
or "not as good as _____. . . ."

Walk slowly to the locker room;
sit down on the bench, feel dejected.
You are all alone. . . .

Then let Jesus come in to the place
where you are locked in to your past disappointments. . . .
Let Him lead you out into the fresh air,
away from that strange city,
up to a high mountain where a chapel is. . . .

It is easy, in this quiet place,
to understand that you are in your Father's Kingdom;
not in the "kingdom" of those who judge you harshly,
comparing you unfavorably to others. . . .

Just be still
and feel the peace of Jesus' presence. . . .

Let Jesus remind you—in His own words—
how He did not let unpopularity
unsettle His confidence in God. . . .

Let Him remind you how you, too, will suffer—
just as He did—
and how you, too,
can draw strength from the self-same prayer as His. . . .

7
Jesus Sees What We Miss

Jesus said to the crowds, "The queen of the south . . .
came from the farthest corner of the world to listen to
the wisdom of Solomon, but you have a greater than
Solomon here . . . At the preaching of Jonah the citi-
zens of Nineveh reformed, but you have a greater than
Jonah here."

Luke 11:29-32

Reflection:

Jesus has a perfect right to complain about His neighbors—
those who should be His friends. They have rejected Him, refused
to listen to Him, because He was too familiar. . . . He "grew up in
their midst."

Jesus reminds them that the Queen of Sheba traveled miles to
listen to Solomon's wisdom; that the Ninevites listened to the
prophet Jonah. Yet Christ's own townspeople refused to learn anything from our Lord.

We are like those people criticized by Jesus, sometimes. Even
when we don't directly refuse to listen to Jesus' words, we do
refuse Him indirectly. Often, it is certain people among our circle
of closest friends, or certain members of our own family, that we
have turned off. (Familiarity breeds contempt.)

It is possible, even now, that we can remember their words or
good example and re-learn their wisdom . . . if only we relax
enough to listen to them. Perhaps we've missed many opportunities for Christ's grace to come to us through these neglected
sources. Perhaps we're missing out on wisdom the same way
Jesus' neighbors did. Just possibly, a "new alertness to those
around us" may come from prayer.

Meditation:

In your imagination,
go to a party given by friends of yours
—friends and those close members of your family. . . .

As you move about from cluster to cluster,
notice the ones you usually pay attention to. . . .
and those you don't. . . .

At last, observe an uninvited guest,
standing over by the curtains, all by Himself.
He allows you to recognize Him as Jesus.

Let Him quietly explain to you
how much you have been missing
by having looked down your nose
at this or that member of your family. . . .
by having ignored the goodness and wisdom
of a taken-for-granted friend. . . .

But let our Lord do more
than speak regretfully of your negligence
that can never be reclaimed.
Let Him tell you of the qualities *He* admires
in those very people that you were too busy,
or too snobbish,
to notice.
Let Him tell you what *He* notices;
and take the time to look at your friends and family
through His eyes. . . .

Finally, let Him suggest ways
that you can now make up for lost time. . . .

8
The Word is Bread, not Stones

Jesus said, "Would one of you hand his son a stone when he asks for a loaf (of bread) ... If you, with all your sins, know how to give your children what is good, how much more will your heavenly Father give good things to anyone who asks him!"

Matt. 7:7-12

Reflection:

Today's Gospel presents one of our Lord's most important instructions on how we are to pray. Jesus would have us remember our kindnesses to other people. We are not to dwell on the times we have sinned against others, or played them false, or hurt their feelings ... or "gave them stones when they asked for bread."

We must confess our sins, of course; we must change our selfish ways. But we are not to "nag ourselves" for the bad side of our nature. We are told to spend more time thinking about the good we have done for others. It is from *these* reflections that we understand how kindly God our Father is ready to treat us.

Notice, Jesus does *not* say, "Remember all the times you have been cruel to others, or selfishly demanding, or thoughtlessly preoccupied—My Father is as cruel and selfish and uncaring as you are at your worst ... only more so!"

This is *not* what Jesus says. Just the opposite. He says, "Remember all the times you have been kind to others, and helped them to live fuller lives, and responded to their needs with thoughtful care. If you, imperfect as you are, can be so good to others, realize that My Father is as kind and as helpful and as responsive as you are at your best ... only more so!"

Jesus instructs us to think of our good side. From this vantage point, we understand that God loves us, constantly and perfectly, in the same way that we love others when we are at our best.

Let this be our evening prayer today—and perhaps every day of our lives. It will not make us complacent. It will give us wiser clues about the nature of God the Father as revealed by Jesus ... and it will increase our motivation to do an even better job of giving bread, not stones, to everyone we meet. Let us pray:

Meditation:

In your imagination,
you are in bed,
or relaxing in a soft chair,
at the end of the day. . . .

Close your eyes.
Imagine a large TV screen in front of you.
Flip the dial to the channel marked: "Good Things I've Done,"
and watch *this* version of your own "11 O'clock News."

Pass in review the day just spent,
starting with the evening,
then suppertime,
late afternoon, early afternoon, lunch break,
morning, and so on. . . .

Remember, in a detached way,
(you are simply an observer, watching yourself on the screen,)
all the good you did for others,
in many little, ordinary ways. . . .

(Don't think of the bad.
It is not the time for this.
Also, don't think of the good things you did
only to make yourself feel bad;
that is, don't think, "I did good for so and so;
why didn't they appreciate it!")

Simply think of the good you did
because it was a good thing to do.
And so you did it. . . .

Then from these memories,
switch the channel to the one that's marked,
"Learning What God Is Like."
That is, make the jump from *your* goodness to *God's*.
He is as good to you as you were to others
—only He is even better! . . . .

Let these thoughts remain with you
until you fall peacefully asleep. . . .

9
Jesus the Reconciler

Jesus said, "If you bring your gift to the altar and there recall that your brother has anything against you, leave your gift at the altar, go first and be reconciled with your brother, and then come and offer your gift."

Matt. 5:20-26

Reflection:

Jesus says hard things about being reconciled before our gifts at the altar will be accepted. He even puts it in the most difficult way: "If your brother has anything against *you!*" (Note: the word "brother" here, as almost always in Sacred Scripture, is taken in the wide sense: "associates professing the same faith," "fellow-citizens of the same country," and even "every human in the world.")

It is hard enough for me to "shake hands and forgive" someone who has hurt *me*. But at least, in this case, I was the person offended . . . so I am in the superior position. I can be noble in my gesture of forgiveness.

But Jesus does not word His warning this way. His words speak of the situation in which I am the *offending* party. I have to ask my neighbor's forgiveness and take the risk that he might either graciously accept my apology . . . or disagreeably insult me as soon as I stick my neck out.

Because of the risk and the possible embarrassment, it is much more difficult to be reconciled when the fault is mine. Perhaps the most practical aspect of this command is lodged in the area of "being reconciled to criticism." Somebody has "something against me" and has told me so. His criticism may not be kind, but it may be true. It may be that I *am* lazy or greedy or preoccupied or opinionated or bothering him in some way.

I hear these criticisms. They bring me up short! It is hard to live with them. It is hard to admit my faults and start improving. It is hard, also, to be reconciled to the critic who brought up these belittling things in the first place.

It is easier to go after the person than to take in what he said. Here is where our Lord's severe warning must apply. Because His warning goes so much against the grain, we need prayer—to quiet down long enough to let God touch us with the humility of reconciliation.

Meditation:

In your imagination,
go to a lovely meadow (or some other outdoor quiet place). . . .
Let the afternoon sun warm your shoulders. . . .
Relax. . . .
Concentrate on the deep rhythm of your breathing. . . .

Remember a person who criticized you recently. . . .
Let this person come to your quiet place.
Continue to be relaxed. . . .
be in control of all anxiety;
try to remain calm. . . .

Let the critic point out your faults in his/her customary way. . . .
Listen to what he has to say,
in the way he usually says it,
without defensiveness. . . .

Then let another person join the two of you.
This one is a friend of yours—
one from whom it is easy to accept advice. . . .

Let your friend point out the same shortcomings of yours,
only let him do it in a more kindly way. . . .
(That is, let your friend be the intermediary of reconciliation
between your critic and yourself. . . .)

Finally, let both friend and critic shake hands
and walk away, out of sight. . . .

In silence, ask God to give you courage
to improve on those aspects of your life
that (thanks to those who "had something against you")
you have discovered are in need of improvement. . . .

10
God's Anti-Perfectionism Campaign

Jesus said, "My command to you is: love your enemies, pray for your persecutors. This will prove that you are sons of your heavenly Father, for his sun rises on the bad and the good, he rains on the just and the unjust. ... In a word, you must be perfect as your heavenly Father is perfect."

Matt. 5:43-48

Reflection:

Along with the "Bread and Stone Teaching" (Recall Chapter 8, page 26), this Gospel is the most moving one for me. Jesus reveals His Father as "the giver of sun and rain" to both the bad and the good. In a practical way, Jesus is launching God's "Anti-Perfectionist Campaign."

True, the last sentence of the Gospel states: "Be perfect, therefore, as your heavenly Father is perfect." But the word, as used by Jesus 20 centuries ago, does not have the same meaning that it has today. Today, "Be perfect!" means "Be faultless!" "Be 100% giving and joyful and at peace ... or else be discontented with self and with others because of the flaws observed!"

Christ's words can't mean this kind of perfectionism. He explains *His* meaning by describing how His Father mercifully bestows the necessary conditions for life on *all* people—bad as well as good, the unjust as well as the just.

God is *thorough* in His love. (Jesus speaks of "perfect" in the sense of "unconditional.") God never holds back the essentials. He is no fierce task-master reserving sun and rain to Himself—then doling these out, as a reward, only for those rare creatures who qualify as blameless individuals. God does not withdraw His grace from those who have not measured up to some standard of perfection. He continues to be kind.

So must we. We, too, must be thorough in our love—not locking anyone out of our care just because he/she has been less-than-perfect in the past. To do this it is necessary that we not lock ourselves out of our own kindness to ourselves just because *we* have been less-than-perfect, too.

It is difficult to do this. There is a harsh spirit within us all that wants to "never let up," to "never forget past faults." We need prayer to let Christ's spirit replace the demon of our drought-producing perfectionism.

Meditation:

In your imagination,
go to a quiet place, on a high hill,
where you can see all of your past life,
year after year,
spread out on the valley below. . . .

Pretend that you are a fierce and vengeful "god"
(It won't be hard to do—
you've often played this role against yourself.)
Take note of some of the glaring imperfections you are guilty of:
your manipulation of others,
mistakes of choice,
self-pity,
lack of courage,
being duped. . . .

Because of all these blemishes in your character,
become extremely displeased with yourself;
and, like an angry god,
punish yourself by blocking off all the sun and rain. . . .

Observe how all that grows in the valley shrivels up.
Feel saddened by all the lack of life that lies below you. . . .
Feel your present hopelessness as well. . . .

Then let the sun break through
and let the gentle rain give relief to the parched land. . . .

Turn and see Jesus coming down from a higher hill.
Let Him quietly relieve you of the burden of "playing god. . . ."

Let Him speak of today's Gospel in His own words.
As He talks to you, watch God's sun and rain
make the valley good and green again. . . .

As you watch, let Jesus point out
some of the interesting scenery in the panorama of your past life:
let Him praise you for the ways you've grown so far,
despite your imperfections. . . .
Let Him remind you that it was God's sun and rain—
His constant presence and assurance—
that has helped you through it all. . . .

Let Him warn you to be as gentle with yourself
as He is, and has always been, with you. . . .

Then let Jesus teach you how to be tolerant with all—
to be just as thorough in your kindness to others
as you have learned to be thorough with yourself. . . .

11
Jesus—True to His Promise

Jesus said, "Give, and it shall be given to you. Good measure pressed down, shaken together, running over, will they pour into the fold of your garment. For the measure you measure with will be measured back to you."

Luke 6:36-38

Reflection:

Christ's message is exuberant today. No mincing with Him! No "exact measure!" No fair wage to balance out a full job! He promises a return for the good we do; and He doesn't count the cost: "Give, and it shall be given back to you." How shall it be given back? *Good* measure, not just adequate, but *good* . . . not simply a fair wage return, but: "pressed down, shaken together, running over," will goodness be poured into your lap!

That's some promise! Why is it that we so seldom experience this "pressed down, shaken together, running over" return of goodness coming back to us after we have done an act of kindness? That is, why don't Christ's promises come true?

Many reasons. One of them is psychological. As a rule, we don't allow this "running over" goodness a chance to be experienced. We have what might be called two "interpretation machines" located somewhere in our brains. One machine registers (and interprets) other people's kindness, thoughtfulness, encouragement, appreciation, etc.—all the good things we receive. This machine is usually rusty. It doesn't function well, or often. We don't pay much attention to it.

The other machine registers (and interprets) other people's meanness, thoughtlessness, rejection, lack-of-appreciation, etc.— all the negative things we receive. This machine is overworked and very, very sensitive.

It's not that the "good measure" of Christ's promises is not going on. It's just that we are not all that aware of it. We need prayer to give at least *equal time* to let our good interpretation machine do what it is supposed to.

Meditation:

In your imagination,
go to a porch that has a happy memory attached to it
(a porch where someone once lived
who had been kind to you. . . .)

Let this person come out to the porch
and sit beside you. . . .
Take the time to express—in your own words—
how much that kindness has meant to you. . . .
Tell the person how you have prayed for him/her,
explain how, in so many ways,
the memory of his goodness has influenced your life. . . .
(The person will be very pleased to hear your words;
by stirring up your gratitude,
you are giving back—
"pressed down, shaken together, running over"—
what he gave you. . . .)

Now let the tables turn:
let this person be a messenger of God,
announcing to you
how the same thing often happened in your life
when *you* were on the giving end.
Quietly, and without argument (or false humility)
let yourself receive these suggestions
about how your helpfulness has influenced other people
in ways that you never thought about. . . .

Stay with this quiet recollection,
prodded by your friend's words,
as long as it seems right to you.
Let yourself receive as much gratitude from others
"pressed down, shaken together, running over"
—as much as you can stand. . . .

At the end,
thank God for whatever insights came.
They are all His gift. . . .

12
Jesus Against Sulking

*Jesus said, "Do not follow the example (of the scribes
and the Pharisees) . . . All their works are performed to
be seen. They are fond of places of honor . . . of marks
of respect . . . The greatest among you will be the one
who serves the rest."*

Matt. 23:1-12

Reflection:

There are two moods that Jesus speaks about in no uncertain
terms. One is a mood He detests. It is a "They-can't-do-this-to-
me" mood—a mood that demands respect, honors, service—the
haughty "demandingness" of the scribes and the Pharisees. Jesus
warns us not to be like that.

The other mood is one of service: "How can I be of help to
you?" No one is praised more highly than the person of this mood.
He or she is, literally, the greatest!

The Pharisee is easily disappointed, easily hurt. He goes
through life cherishing the constant expectation, "Other people
ought to serve *me, my* way!" Such a demand seldom gets obeyed;
it never does for long. And so the Pharisee ends up grumbling that
he doesn't get any respect.

The giving person is never cheated out of anything, for his idea
is to help, and not to *be* helped.

Perhaps, in practical terms, not many people today lord it over
others in the grand style of putting unreasonable demands on people. We are more sneaky than that. Most often, the "Pharisee
mood" attacks us *after* the fact, when we get discouraged by the
lack of appreciation for something we've already done.

Most people are good people. Most people really do love; they
are good and kind in the spontaneous impulse of kindness. Most
people, ourselves included, are not like arrogant kings expecting
others to be our fawning subjects.

But we are—often enough—like sulking kings-in-exile who complain when others do not fawn with some preconceived display of humble gratitude . . . "after all we've done for them!" This is being pharisaical *after* the fact, but it is still Phariseeism! "All their works are performed to be seen." Prayer is needed to get us over the "after-hurts."

Meditation:

In your imagination,
take yourself to your favorite "Sulking corner. . . ."
Return again to a recent time
when you were disappointed by somebody's lack
of respect or appreciation. . . .

Feel the mood of righteous indignation once again.
Then *exaggerate* it—"blow yourself up" even more. . . .
dress yourself with fancy clothes (like the Pharisees);
put on a heavy medal that says, "I should be served by others!"

Take a good look at yourself—
your pout, your fancy clothes, the ugly medal—
take a good look, and have a good laugh at your expense. . . .

Then leave your corner, going at your own pace,
and relax in a comfortable chair. . . .
Let Jesus enter through the locked doors of your sulking room.
Let Him take off that heavy medal
and put it out of sight, in whatever way He chooses to. . . .

Let Him take off your rich robe,
replacing it with a servant's garment, one just like His. . . .

Remain with Him in silence.
It may very well be
that He will want to tell you where . . .
                        and how . . .
                        and whom you are to serve. . . .
                        and why. . . .

13
Jesus Reroutes Our Preoccupations

The mother of (James and John) asked Jesus, "Promise me that these sons of mine will sit, one at your right hand and the other at your left." In reply, Jesus said (to James and John), "You do not know what you are asking. Can you drink of the cup I am to drink of?" "We can," they said. He told them, "... you shall ..."

Matt. 20:17-28

Reflection:

Prayer, when it has a lot of expectation to it, has a way of confusing the *product* with the *process.*

We ask God for help, or patience, or wisdom, or tolerance. These are all *process* graces—qualities of mind and heart that enable us to work through the situations life hands out to us.

But then our impatient hearts quickly turn our requests from the qualities we need to the results we want. The *help* we pray for turns into a list of specifics: "... so that I can attain this goal or be freed from that burden!" *Patience* turns into something like, "... so that Mr. _____ won't hassle me on the job!" *Wisdom* turns into "... so that I will possess the magic solution to this specific problem!" *Tolerance* turns into "... so that nothing and nobody will bother me any more!"

James and John, and the mother of the two Apostles were not very concerned about process (Carrying their cross, serving others, drinking from the cup of salvation—God's will—one day at a time.) At least in this Gospel passage, they seem to be concentrating on results—the *product*—rewards—"Sitting in Glory beside Jesus Christ in His Kingdom."

Jesus re-routed their preoccupation. The reward, the final result of their prayers, was not His to give. God the Father is in charge of the final results. Our Lord's concern and His promise focused on *process:* "Anyone who aspires to be great must serve the rest" ... "Grace will be supplied to enable you to be like Me."

Let us ask for the grace of today's Gospel to heal the impatient spirit in us.

Meditation:

In your imagination,
go to a good place that you remember—
a "place apart"
(perhaps a little room you had when you made a good retreat,
or when you enjoyed a pleasurable vacation). . . .
You are alone, and happy to be so. . . .

Remember a situation that discouraged you recently—
somebody let you down,
a problem wasn't solved,
a plan did not come through as you had hoped. . . .

Write two letters to Jesus:
in one letter, write up the remembered situation
simply from the standpoint of *product*. . . .
(This will be easy to do.
It needs no prayer at all.
Considering the results, it was a failure;
considering your feelings about it, you are sad.)

"Mail" this letter,
expecting no more of a reply—and no less!—
than James and John received.

Then write a second letter,
remember the situation from the standpoint of *process*—
what you learned
about suffering,
about your own limited abilities,
about compassion for others who are in the same boat,
whatever else. . . .

"Mail" this letter, too.
You can expect a response from this one.
Jesus may want to write a letter back,
filling you in on things you may have missed.

Give time for this possibility. . . .

14
Jesus on "Ups and Downs"

Jesus said, "Once there was a rich man . . . who died and was buried. . . . He called out, 'Father Abraham, have pity on me. Send Lazarus to dip the tip of his finger in water to refresh my tongue, for I am tortured in these flames.' 'My child,' replied Abraham, 'remember that you were well off in your lifetime, while Lazarus was in misery. Now he has found consolation, but you have found torment.' "

Luke 16:19-31

Reflection:

So many things change. Thrilling experiences, which meant the world to us, turn out to be sawdust in the mouth. This applies not only to the addict or the alcoholic; it applies to all the lively ventures that have promise of quick results or chemical peace or easy pleasure. It is true of the rich man in today's Gospel. A year-long pleasure does not always tell the whole story.

The other way around is also true. Lazarus, even in his misery, ended up happy and content—a bosom-friend of Abraham. Similar things have happened to us. A period of depression, a series of rejections that made the heart sick, a fall from grace (or from luck) that sorely tested the will to live . . . these have often been the times for truth-facing, without which we would have stagnated.

A drinker, starting out, is happy—as the rich man was having a good time every day; soon he is hooked and wastes his life until he hits bottom; then something happens to change him—he reaches for grace. Afterwards, he can look back at the lowest point of his degradation and see it as the beginning phase of a new life. It is also the place where he gains wisdom; he can now help others. Being a "familiar of the territory," he can be compassionate to others who are suffering as he has suffered.

Up is down sometimes—and down is the beginning of up. The rich and merry go broke, and the poor in spirit are blessed. Perhaps you have experienced this already. Perhaps it may even be so for you right now. Grace may be speaking to your heart.

Meditation:

In your imagination,
get into your favorite car. . . .
(If you have never driven a car,
imagine you are riding with a chauffeur
who is completely trustworthy. . . .)

As you drive along,
think of the "downer" times in your life:
see if you can discover a *pattern* in these times—
a certain set of circumstances,
or a certain type of person,
that seems to be the recurrent cause of your "downer. . . ."

Up ahead on the road,
you notice Jesus, hitch-hiking. . . .
Stop the car;
invite Him to sit beside you. . . .

As you drive along,
tell Him about what you've been thinking. . . .
how, so very often in your life,
there seems to be a "favorite way" for you to get discouraged—
and how there seems to be a pattern, also,
in the way that you "bounce back."

Ask our Lord to give you more wisdom about this pattern:
how you can control your "downers" well enough
so that they don't devastate you—
and so that you can cooperate more fully
in the "Lazarus-like situations"
of coming back to life again. . . .

Let Jesus speak to your silence
with His understanding of "ups" and "downs. . . ."
and His wisdom about which is which. . . .

15
Jesus on Anger

Jesus said to the chief priests and elders of the people: "Listen to this parable. There was a property owner who planted a vineyard. . . Then he leased it out to tenant farmers and went on a journey. When vintage time arrived he . . . finally sent his son, thinking, 'They will respect my son.' When they saw the son, the tenants said to one another, 'Here is the one who will inherit everything. Let us kill him . . .'."

Matt. 21:33-46

Reflection:

It is difficult to control any of our emotions; and the most difficult for most of us is anger. Usually, we get entrenched in one extreme or the other—we either swallow all our anger and frustration so that the adversary never knows how we feel; or else we "lay it all out" with such an onslaught of vented irritation that the adversary really has no choice but to remain in fierce opposition.

Jesus was more balanced, more "anger-disciplined." He told the chief priests and the elders where He stood and how He felt about the way they were trying to trap Him. He did not pretend He was not angry. He *was* angry; and He cared enough about His enemies to let them know it.

Even so, Jesus did not let them know it in such a way as to freeze them into opposition. He expressed Himself by means of a parable. This way, they had a chance to think about their behavior and to change their attitude toward Jesus, if they wanted to. (Who knows, maybe it did do some good—maybe Joseph of Arimathea had a change of heart that began on the very day he heard this story of the wicked vine-dressers.)

Our Lord had the right balance. We need His Spirit—we need more balance in the way we express anger and hurt feelings. We need to have Christ's combination of composure, courage and compassion.

It would be a good thing for all of us to pray for . . . to quietly prepare for the possibility that God's Spirit may be wanting to help us with the right management of our lives; if only we can be still, and gently quiet down the false urgencies of our hearts.

Meditation:

In your imagination,
take yourself to a kitchen that has pleasant associations. . . .
You are alone,
sitting at the kitchen table,
having a cup of coffee. . . .

Think of some recent situation
that has upset you or hurt your feelings in some way. . . .

Let two "spirits" come out of you—out either ear:

First: The "Spirit of Repressed Anger"
    —that shy side of you
    which warns you not to say anything;
    just swallow your hurt feelings
    and continue to feel sorry for yourself!

Second: The "Spirit of Unchecked Anger"
    —that vengeful side of you
    which urges you to retaliate against,
    nag at,
    or somehow crush whoever it was that hurt you. . . .

Listen—*really* listen—
to what each has to say.
Pay attention to your feelings
as you are being influenced by their advice. . . .

Then order them both out of the room.
Send them off;
and tell them not to slam the door on their way out. . . .

Pay attention to how you feel now,
with those two manipulators gone. . . .

Then let Jesus enter.
Let Him sit beside you at the kitchen table
and give you good advice,
in whatever way He chooses,
on how to express your anger
openly,
honestly,
prudently,
and in a way that has a chance to heal. . . .

16
Jesus on Pouting

The tax-collectors and sinners were all gathering around Jesus to hear him, at which the Pharisees and the scribes murmured, "This man welcomes sinners and eats with them." At this Jesus addressed this parable to them: "A man had two sons . . . meanwhile the elder son was out on the land. As he neared the house on his way home, he heard the sound of music and dancing. He . . . would not go in; but his father came out and began to plead with him . . . 'My son, you are with me always and everything I have is yours. But we must celebrate and rejoice! This brother of yours was dead, and has come back to life.' "

Luke 15:1-3, 11-32

Reflection:

The Parable of the Prodigal Son is probably Christ's best-known story. Most people identify with the younger brother—the Prodigal who returned to his father and was not only reinstated, but even honored with a homecoming party as though he were a hero.

Meditating on the parable from this point of view does have its benefits. It is always a good idea to reawaken our gratitude to God for His marvelous treatment of us. Not only does He forgive us our sins; but He does so in a most delicate way—God makes us feel good about coming home to Him instead of making us feel badly about our going away in the first place.

But the parable has a lesson—a *strong* lesson—as well as motives for gratitude. To hear the lesson, we must identify with the *older* brother—that character who was like the Pharisees Jesus was talking to.

The Pharisees were envious of the "other people" who seemed to be on such good terms with Jesus. They murmured about our Lord's apparent lack of discriminating taste. They grumbled that too much respect was given to people whom they judged to be unworthy of respect.

Sometimes we are more like the older brother than the prodigal. Not always, of course—sometimes. It may be that a fellow-worker is honored, or given a raise, and we feel we deserved it more. "It's not fair!" It may be that a neighbor gets a big break, perhaps wins a lottery, even though he treats his family shabbily and is irresponsible. "It's not fair!" It may be that a dissolute member of our family has been generously remembered in grandfather's will—maybe more generously than we were—even though we did much more for grandfather than he ever did. "It's not fair!"

It is at these times that we should identify with the older brother, who felt sorry for himself and sulked outside while people were celebrating the good fortune of somebody else. Let prayer come to us . . . let Jesus come to us . . . in this mood:

Meditation:

In your imagination,
stand outside a house where a party is going on:
friend, family, fellow-worker . . . whoever . . .
is being honored and admired. . . .

And you don't like it.
You have been passed over, not appreciated!
The "other" is getting all the breaks and recognition.
You are sulking. . . .
Bring back to your memory
a time when you actually *did* sulk like this.
Stay with this miserable feeling for a while . . .

Then let Jesus leave the house
and come outside to see you.
He asks you, "What's the matter?"
Tell Him
(just the way you've rehearsed it so often
within your embittered heart). . . .

Then let Jesus say to you
what He said to the older brother in the Gospel.
Let Him remind you
how much He loves you. . . .
how you have not been forgotten,
just because He honors other people too. . . .

Let Jesus praise you for all the good you've done,
for all your faithfulness. . . .

Then permit Jesus
to persuade you—in His own words—
to let Him love whomever *He* wants to love—
in whatever way *He* chooses. . . .

17
The Courage of Jesus—
Ours for the Asking

When Jesus had come to Nazareth, he said to the people in the synagogue: "No prophet gains acceptance in his native place . . ." At these words the whole audience in the synagogue was filled with indignation. They rose up and expelled him from the town, leading him to the brow of the hill . . . intending to hurl him over the edge. But he went straight through their midst and walked away.

Luke 4:24-30

Reflection:

Winston Churchill wrote a history about the events leading up to World War II. He called it *The Gathering Storm*. In a similar way, Holy Mother Church presents her "accumulated evidence" in many of the Gospels of Lent—the "gathering storm" of hatred and treachery which led to the crucifixion of Jesus Christ our Lord.

Jesus knew what was going on. He could not do much about it. He could not be true to His Father's will and, at the same time, please those who wanted their Messiah to be a militant leader, not the Prince of Peace. They "led Him to the brow of the hill, intending to hurl Him over the edge. But He went straight through their midst and walked away."

We all have our share of treacherous opponents. Each has a different set of them, but we all have some. They, too, would like us to be defeated somehow.

It would be so easy to buckle under their pressure. It is so difficult to keep our courage up. There is a part of us that could readily let ourselves be pushed off the brow of that precipice. At least, that way, peace would come—no more struggle, no more facing up to antagonism—death, or any kind of *giving up*, could end a lot of hurts.

It is at these times that we need prayer most of all. We need the grace that comes especially from today's Gospel—the dauntless courage of Jesus Christ, able to turn away from the precipice of despairing thoughts and walk straight through the glare of other people's hatred and dislike.

Meditation:

In your imagination,
start walking slowly up an old dirt road.
Your shoulders are slumped, as though you carry a burden;
your steps are uneasy. . . .

Beside every clump of bush,
you hear your enemies speaking hard things against you;
or talking about you, disdainfully, to the others. . . .
Remember some real occasions
when people actually did talk behind your back,
or showed their hatred of you,
or gave you a "put down."
Wince, once more, from the hurt of those occasions.
Let them come to life again as you keep walking. . . .

Approach the brow of a hill where the dirt road ends.
Understand that your enemies (or gossips)
want you to end it all. . . .

Then notice Jesus,
walking down to you from a higher hill. . . .

Wait for Him
—do not look down!—
do not think about leaping into despair. . . .

Let Jesus take your hand. . . .
Together, you walk back,
straight through the midst of your enemies. . . .

Let His courage be passed on to you:
feel the warmth of it coming from His hand;
feel the weight on your shoulders lighten;
feel the spring in your steps come back. . . .

Continue walking hand in hand
until you are comforted and strong again . . .
as long as it seems good to do so. . . .

18
Jesus on Forgiveness

Peter came up and asked Jesus, "Lord, when my brother wrongs me, how often must I forgive ... ?" Jesus replied, "The reign of God may be likened to a king who ... wrote off a large debt of his servant. The servant then siezed and throttled those who owed him money. The king was angry and said: 'You worthless wretch! I canceled your entire debt when you pleaded with me. Should you not have dealt mercifully with your fellow servant, as I have dealt with you?' "

Matt. 18:21-35

Reflection:

Forgiveness is the ultimate test of a Christian. Jesus saw to it that both the act *and* the attitude of forgiveness is given prime consideration.

Christ's revelation is, for the most part, a message that elicits love, not fear. His Gospel is one that renews hope, assures joy, replaces anxiety with confidence in God. But in this one area of *remembered grudges,* Christ's message is one of frightening severity: "My Father will hand you over to the torturers unless each of you forgives his brother from his heart!"

This is a hard saying. Of all the lessons of our Lord, this is the area where we especially would like a "lightness of touch" from Jesus, and a lot of loopholes. For the fact is that we prefer to dwell upon remembered hurts and past rejections ... and yet we still want to be considered Christian. If only Jesus were not so severe about this command, we could make a good case for ourselves for being *not* obliged to keep the law of forgiveness. We insist that we have good cause for forgiving, but not forgetting! At the very least we cling to our need to keep stewing about it, nursing the wound, not letting the injury be healed.

A person could have been kind to us for years, providing us with

many hours of a listening ear and compassionate counsel. Then—
just once! —let this person *not* be available and we feel cut off. We
promptly forget past favors; we feel slighted by that person's
change of heart.

A Catholic could have gone to confession 200 times in his or
her life. God's forgiveness and the priest's absolution were grace-
filled experiences. On the 201st time, the penitent met up with a
stern, bad-tempered priest for a confessor. From then on, the one
bad experience outweighed all the good ones.

And on it goes. One unanswered prayer and God is impatiently
dismissed. One mean teacher in grammar school and nuns are no
longer good. One rejection from a friend and friend is friend no
more.

We forget, as did the servant in today's Gospel. The *huge*
amount of mercy shown to us—and we are prepared to throttle
those who owe us in some way. It no longer matters that their
"debt"—their meanness to us—is but a small fraction of the mer-
cies we have "lifetimely" received.

It is necessary to remember that God is not *only* a God of mercy
and forebearance. He is also a God of justice—fierce and insis-
tent—on this one point in particular: "forgiving one another from
our hearts."

Meditation:

In your imagination,
go to a courthouse.
Give yourself the role of judge,
robes and all. . . .

The accused enters:
a person
who has hurt you.
This person is the cause of your feeling injured, somehow. . . .

Put this person,
and the injury he caused,
on the "minus side" of a large scale
placed in the middle of the courtroom.

Notice how the balance goes against him. . . .
(This is how you normally view the case. . . .)

Then remember all the times the same person
has been kind to you. . . .
Put this on the other scale—the "plus side. . . ."

Then remember other people,
all through your life,
who have been kind to you. . . .
(Ask the Holy Spirit to help you here—
the tendency is to load the scales
with memories of people who were mean to you.
Resist this temptation. . . .)

At this point,
let Jesus enter the courtroom.
He first goes over to the "plus side" of the scales
and places a life-sized crucifix,
with the same weight of His original cross;
and the same weight of His real dead body,
given up for love of you. . . .
Observe how the scales now show where the weight is. . . .

Then invite Jesus
to replace you as judge of the whole matter. . . .
(He is going to do so anyway;
but it would be better if you asked Him to. . . .)

He does not let you stay in the room.
He will judge in His own way,
in His own time,
without your counsel. . . .

Finally, let Jesus join you outside the courtyard.
Nothing is said of the past experience.
Let Him talk to you
about some things He wants you to be doing. . . .

19
Jesus on What Can and Can't Be Changed

Jesus said to his disciples: "Do not think that I have come to abolish the law and the prophets. I have come, not to abolish them, but to fulfill them."

Matt. 5:17-19

Reflection:

Jesus, today, declares Himself to be the fulfiller of traditions. He did not abolish the law. He did see fit to change, or ignore, many of the regulations that surrounded the law. He often innovated—expressing the spirit of Moses and the prophets in different ways.

This was the favorite complaint the Pharisees had against Him. *They* thought He was a renegade, a revolutionary; *He* knew He was not.

The law and the prophets demanded that the Chosen People cultivate certain moral and religious responses—these responses were considered necessary signs of their faithfulness to God. Jesus declared that He brought these responses to fulfillment in Himself. Our Lord did not observe all the culturally acquired methods for putting these responses into action. He did not follow all the fasting regulations, for instance, Jesus permitted the disciples to eat corn as they walked on the Sabbath. The precise ways that laws were expressed and experienced—these changed. But Jesus did not alter—He *perfected!*—the basic statutes which spelled out the ideals of love, mercy, gratitude, and justice of the heart.

So with us. The Church has changed through the centuries; each generation has expressed different "styles" in its faithful response to God.

This is true, not only for the Church; it is also true for every individual. We have a certain way, now, of "putting flesh" on the qualities of kindness, patience, courage, service to others, etc. The way we do it now is different from our style of kindness and the

like as we expressed it ten years ago . . . from our style as teenagers . . . from our style as children.

So often, we get unnecessarily discouraged because we have not
lived up to the ideals we used to have. These ideals, so often, we
dreamed up in our adolescence and glued together with specific
demands that came to be unreachable.

The ideal was to "do something with my life" . . . to "be kind to
others" . . . to "be somebody, noteworthy and heroic." These are
fine. But the way these noble goals were wished for were all bound
up with hero-worship and daydreaming and that impossible self-
demand that we must never be anything less than perfect.

Many people are heroic just keeping the family together; they
are not heroic as Joan of Arc was. Many people are kind and unselfish in little ways; they are not Tom Dooley or Theresa of Avila.
Many religious are living good lives, inspired by the spirit of their
founder; but they are not observing the mode of dress or prayer or
preaching that the founder had originally observed.

It would be well to pray for Christ's instruction,—hoping to understand, from Him, what the difference is between the demands
on us which cannot be changed and the variety of ways that these
demands can be expressed.

Meditation:

In your imagination,
go to an easy chair
in a comfortable room. . . .

Call up the "Ghost of your own Past"—
let your "Ghost" remind you
of the *qualities*—kind, unselfish, caring, etc.—
that you wanted your life to be. . . .

Then call up the "Good Ghost of the Present". . . .
(Make sure it is the *Good* one, not the Bad one.)

Let both "Ghosts" share ideas with each other. . . .
Notice how well the two of them get along. . . .
Pay attention to what you may have been missing:

how, in so many little, hidden ways,
"Present Life" is really fulfilling the ideals of "Past Hopes". . . .

(Don't you say anything . . .
        Let your "Good Ghost of the Present" do most of
        the talking.
        If the "Ghost of the Past"
        starts enumerating all the failures and mistakes
        that you have made,
        gently explain
        that these things have been brought up
        many, many times before.
        Let the Good Ghost remind him
        that, "Right now,
        we're talking about the simple, ordinary ways
        in which the ideal of goodness and the law of love
        have been lived out.")

Finally, let Jesus come into the room
and give you hints
about how the "Ghosts of the Future"
might take shape. . . .

Let Him advise you
about how you can help this process. . . .

20
Jesus' Answer to Backbiting Criticism

Jesus was casting out a devil which was mute, and when the devil was cast out the dumb man spoke. The crowds were amazed at this. But some of them said, "It is by Beelzebub, the prince of devils, that he casts out devils."

Luke 11:14-23

Reflection:

In the course of His active ministry, Jesus had to suffer a lot of grief. Most of the time, He could not do much about it. He simply had to take it. He suffered a *psychological* passion long before the excruciating events of Holy Week.

Today's Gospel documents one of the most difficult sorrows Christ was subjected to. He was going about doing good; as He did so, he healed a man who was unable to speak—"Casting out the devil who was mute so that the dumb man spoke."

Most of the people marvelled at what they saw taking place; they praised God for this act of healing goodness worked among them. But some of the crowd interpreted an evil motive into the goodness they could not argue with: "By Beelzebub, the prince of devils, He casts out devils!" Beelzebub (or Beelzebul) was the kingpin of the power of evil—the "devil of devils," so to speak. In today's terminology, Christ's vicious and jealous enemies would say, "Yes, Jesus is doing good with His healing power, but He's doing this in order to manipulate the people—in order to have them in His control!"

We, too, have suffered from the same kind of psychological second-guessing. We have suffered the same kind of "psychological passion." It is difficult to "hang in there" when people attribute bad motives for the very good we do. They see the kind acts we perform—they admit this much—but then they place an ulterior motive on them. They see a selfish reason for the good we do:

> "It's just for show . . ."
> "It's done so that she can manipulate others . . ."
> "He is aligned with the Prince of Power so that he can draw impressionable people into his control . . ."

Nothing much we can do about such backbiting criticism. We can only react the way Jesus did—we can reply that, "If good was done, then it was the hand of God, not the power of evil, that was present."

We can do this . . . we can also pray:

Meditation:

In your imagination,
go to a kindergarten (one that you remember)
and sit on the floor
in the middle of the room. . . .

Remember two or three occasions in your recent years
when you did a good thing for people:
gave money to a charity,
sponsored a good cause,
accepted the hard work of guiding an organization,
volunteered for something,
went out of your way to help someone, somehow. . . .

Think of this;
then let gossips fill in the chairs,
in a full circle,
around you. . . .

Remember what they said about you
and how they said it. . . .
Or imagine them now repeating to your face
the slurs they spoke behind your back. . . .
Let them,
with vicious tongues and mean faces,
put false judgments on your generous acts of kindness. . . .

Feel the sting of their words.
As you do, feel smaller and smaller:
as helpless as a kindergarten child
in the middle of a ring of bullets. . . .

Then let Mary enter the room.
She talks—one at a time—
to each accuser,
sending them off on their own tasks.
(You cannot hear her advice to them.
It comes to you as mumbling.
But they seem to understand.
They forget about you and leave quietly. . . .)

Then Mary sits beside you—just the two of you. . . .
She praises you for the way you resemble her Son. . . .
She points out, in her own gentle way,
other opportunities
for you to continue doing good works in the future. . . .

21
Jesus—Teacher of Love

The scribe said to Jesus: "Excellent, Teacher! you are right in saying, 'God is the One, there is no other than he.' Yet, 'to love him with all our heart, with all our thought and with all our strength, and to love our neighbor as ourselves' is worth more than any burnt offering or sacrifice." Jesus approved the insight of this answer and told him, "You are not far from the reign of God."

Mark 12:28-34

Reflection:

This Gospel could be used for the "Feast of God the Encourager." A lawyer of our Lord's day asked Jesus about the law. Jesus replied. The man was obviously impressed by the way that love of God and love of neighbor were linked.

His response wasn't exactly a "backslapper," but he did show enthusiasm, and he did add something: "This love is better than any routine act of piety, like burnt offerings or mumbled words!"

It was then Jesus' turn to praise. Commending the man, He encouraged him—"He approved the insight of this answer and told him 'You are not far from the kingdom of God.'" It's almost as if Jesus said: "So far, so good, friend. Your understanding is fine. Now get your will into action and put your insights into practice."

Jesus continues His work of encouragement. Whenever we, by meditation, understand the words of God in the Scriptures . . . and whenever we understand the action of God in nature or in ordinary events . . . we, too, receive our Lord's heartwarming approval of our insights.

Jesus also continues to give us a "so far, so good—now get to work at it!" guidance. The best way that He does this is quietly— in solitude with us—when we have put ourselves into that *readiness for God's possibilities* which is the spirit of prayer:

Meditation:

In your imagination,
go to a lovely meadow:
there is a favorite tree (favorite to your memory)
on the top of the hillside. . . .
You feel good.
Lean back against the tree;
imagine yourself opening a book
entitled, "Some Insights I Have Had
About God's Love and About My Love for Others."

As you browse through the pages
remember some of your good inspirations,
from childhood right up to the present. . . .
Stay with this as long as it is productive. . . .

Then close the book
and walk up a high mountain,
over and up from your hillside. . . .
When you get there,
take time to enjoy the beautiful panorama.
Notice that the same kind of tree is up here, too.
Relax against it in the same way. . . .

You sense that Jesus has just left a chapel
farther back from where you are.
He advances toward you until He is on the same overlook.
He sits down beside the same tree. . . .

Gently and kindly,
He encourages you for your understanding and insights.
Let Him warm your heart. . . .

Then let Him advise you
how to put these insights into practice,
charging your will
with whatever challenge He wishes you to hear:
("So far, so good;
now get to work on this. . . .")

22
Jesus on Making Comparisons

Jesus spoke this parable addressed to those who believed in their own self-righteousness while holding everyone else in contempt: "Two men went . . . to pray; one was a Pharisee, the other a tax collector. The Pharisee with head unbowed prayed in this fashion: 'I give you thanks, O God, that I am not like the rest of men . . .' The other . . . said, 'O God, be merciful to me, a sinner.'"

Luke 18:9-14

Reflection:

Like so many familiar things, today's parable about the Pharisee and the Publican (tax-collector) is so well known that we may easily miss the point of the story.

Many people know the poses of the two characters better than they know Christ's purpose in telling the story. There is the "bad guy"—the big braggart dressed in finery, showing off his religiosity in the front pew, pretending to be "holier than thou," complacent in the conviction that he performs more good works and lives more decently than those "nobodys" in the back rows.

Then there is the "good guy" in the back—doubled over, meek as a lamb, not doing anything—small, shy, undistinguished, waiting for God to have mercy on him, a sinner.

Unfortunately, at times, these two roles get turned around: the man in the back becomes the braggart; while the man up front is assumed to be insincere, no matter what he does.

Many Christians believe they are "good guys" if they insist on doing nothing, if they remain as inconspicuous as possible. They take the last pew in Church (if they get there at all), contribute neither energy nor enthusiasm for any Christian work of mercy . . . and all the time proclaiming themselves "more sincere than those do-gooders who are trying to accomplish something with their faith!" ("I may be a no-good sinner, but I'm better than those hypocrites in the limelight . . . I thank thee, Lord, that I am not as phoney as those people who are still trying!")

The point of Christ's parable is that it is wrong to make comparisons . . . *either* way. Only God is judge. It is wrong to think that self is better, or more sincere, than anyone else; it is also wrong to think that self is *not* as good, or as attractive, or as powerful, or as sincere as anyone else.

It is wrong to work *comparison* into the picture in *any* way. Let us pray that God will give us good "preventive medicine":

Meditation:

In your imagination,
take yourself to a small upstairs room
in a modern television station.
It is a cutting room
where reels of film
are shortened, sliced and fitted back together.
There are many, many reels of film stacked on top of each other
—all of them are film-clips about you,
and about the people who have come in and out of your life. . . .

Take out the films of those people
you feel that you are "better than":
(the people you complain about so often
because of their dullness or imperfections
or some other way they haven't measured up
to the standard you have set for them. . . .)
Play enough of these reels of other people's inferiority
until you get tired of it. . . .

Then re-play the films of some of the people
you feel you are "not as good as":
(those who get you down
because, for some reason,
you feel not as joyful or peaceful or patient
or rich or wise or whatever . . .)

Play enough of these
until you get (as usual) quite discouraged. . . .

Notice how frustrated and unhappy you are
from all this work of watching. . . .
Become uncomfortable by the room's dinginess and darkness
—its musty smell and cinematic unreality. . . .

Then take yourself outdoors,
into the clean air,
away from the place of roles and reels. . . .

Just be yourself.
Let two or three people join you,
people you can just be yourself with. . . .

Then let Jesus join you;
have a picnic together. . . .
And, (if He cares to)
let Him speak to you about the week ahead. . . .
suggesting, perhaps,
how good your life can be
if you let it be uncluttered by comparisons. . . .

23
Jesus on Persevering in Prayer

Jesus replied, "Unless you people see signs and won-
ders, you do not believe." "Sir," the royal official
pleaded with him, "come down before my child dies."
Jesus told him, "Return home. Your son will live." The
man put his trust in the words Jesus spoke to him . . .
                                        John 4:43-54

Reflection:

Often enough, prayer is a discouraging thing. This is so both
with the prayer of praise and the prayer of petition. Sometimes, of
course, it is easy to praise the Lord—when a sudden happiness
spontaneously evokes thankfulness to God. This kind of prayer is
not so easy, though, when the mind is strumming on the guitar of
sadness or indignation.

In the same way, prayer of petition is easy at a time of immedi-
ate concern or crisis—an accident, an overwhelming challenge, an
unexpected problem, things like these. At such times, it is natural,
almost instinctive, to pray.

It is when prayer seems to go unanswered—the sickness lingers
on; the problem becomes a long, drawn-out affair without relief;
the person prayed for never seems to change—these are the circumstances that make it difficult to pray.

Persevering in the prayer of petition, *in spite of no apparent*
answer, is the test. We must somehow be like the royal official in
today's Gospel who, although Jesus seemed not to comply with
the prayer that He come down to heal his son—in spite of this, the
man put his trust in Jesus.

Meditation:

Think of the people
—the very special people—
whom you have prayed for, for a long, long time. . . .

In your imagination,
put them all in your house.
Make them feel comfortable. . . .

Tell them that you are going to meet Jesus soon.
In the course of your visit,
you are going to put in a good word for them,
and pray that Jesus heal them. . . .

Ask them to tell you what you should ask Jesus.
Ask them for the right things to pray for. . . .
Try not to put words in their mouths.
Relax.
Be alert.
Remain passive, so that they can tell you
what they need, and how they need it.
Spend as much time as necessary. . . .
Don't be surprised
if, perhaps, their own way of expressing themselves
is different from the way
you usually express your concern for them. . . .

Then leave the house;
meet Jesus and Mary on a favorite street. . . .

Ask our Lord's help for your friends,
wording your requests
as closely as you can remember
in the way they expressed themselves to you. . . .

Ask Mary if you left anything out;
let her respond (if she cares to). . . .

Then let Jesus respond to your prayers
with words, or gestures, or silence,
or whatever He decides on. . . .
Remain in His Presence as long as profitable. . . .

Then go back home
and report to your friends. . . .

24
Jesus on "Busybodies"

Jesus, who knew (the man) had been sick for a long time, said, "Do you want to be healed?" "Sir," the man answered, "I don't have anyone to plunge me into the pool . . . By the time I get there, someone else has gone in ahead of me."

John 5:1-16

Reflection:

Personally, my vote for the "Person I'd Rather *Not* Meet" in all of Scripture is the character—the old crab—who was sick for 38 years and hanging around the Sheep Pool of Jerusalem.

Today's Gospel records his ill-humored characteristics. Jesus asked him if he wanted to be healed. His response was not: "Yes, I do," or "Wow, thanks!," or anything like that. Matter of fact, he didn't even *see* who Jesus was, even though our Lord talked to him and healed him!

All the man did was complain. Instead of admitting that he wanted to be healed, he griped about all the young whippersnappers who beat him to the pool at "healing time."

We know the type—"Everybody else gets the breaks but me!" Of course we know the type. We fit that type ourselves, sometimes. Not always . . . sometimes . . . (in your life and in mine) . . . we spend our time and energy irritating the wounds of our old hurts and keeping alive our indignation over somebody else's preferred treatment. And all the while the Holy Spirit of Jesus is offering us His healing grace and His gift of life and fuller joy.

The work of prayer is to rid ourselves of these ill-humored complaints preoccupying our attention. Once this business (and "busybodiness") is ushered out of our minds, we can then attend to the presence of Jesus asking us: "Never mind about others—what is it that *you* want?"

Meditation:

In your imagination,
go to a busy swimming pool.
It is mid-afternoon, muggy, and uncomfortable. . . .
Noisy children are annoying you;

it seems like everyone's radio is turned up, high,
playing the kind of music that irritates you. . . .
Bugs are fierce,
sun is hot,
noise is deafening,
poolside characters boisterous and obnoxious. . . .

Let this scene represent all the people and things
that bother you most. . . .

Let go of this imaginative scene;
detach yourself from it.
Leave the pool—simply walk away, out of sight. . . .
Let yourself meet Mary;
let her invite you
to a quiet Mass in a lovely chapel in the silent woods. . . .

As you and Mary walk along,
you come upon a still pool,
made by the mountain stream. . . .

Rest awhile—
simply enjoying the quiet together
or talking about things as they come to mind quite naturally. . . .
Stay with this scene as long as it seems right to do so. . . .

Then let Jesus catch up to you.
He asks you, "What do you want Me to do for you?"
Tell Him, in your own words. . . .

Give Jesus a chance to reply, if He wants to.
(He may want to just "be there,"
enjoying the place with Mary and you. . . .)

Finally, when it seems right to do so,
all three of you continue into the woods
to where the chapel is. . . .
and celebrate Holy Mass together. . . .

25
Jesus—Forgiver of Our Sins

Jesus said: "The Father himself judges no one, but has assigned all judgment to the Son . . ."

John 5:17-30

Reflection:

Most people fear judgment as much as they fear death. Both are mysterious. They signify a certain finality—a "once and for all"—an interruption of the familiar . . . and often, bad, bad news.

Most people link God the Father with other harsh, dissatisfied authority figures in their lives. "Good" was "Not enough!" "Excellent" was "What took you so long!" There were thousands of ways to earn the disapproval of authority figures; there were very few ways to please them (and even fewer ways to please them for very long).

Perhaps this is why the words of Jesus in today's Gospel are so encouraging, so reassuring. We are often confused in our understanding of God the Father. God realizes this; He does not demand that we shift the gears of understanding too much. God the Father lets us sift out all the bad memories of harsh judgment by authority figures so that we can realize how God is much more merciful than our unpleasant memories of the past.

God the Father simply hands over to Jesus all power to judge. Though He is God, Jesus is also human, just as human as we are . . . with all His memories of how difficult it is to be human. Simon Peter, James and John fell asleep when Jesus asked them to stay alert during that long night in Gethsemane. Jesus did not deal with them severely. Simon Peter then ran away and, with a blasphemy, three times denied his Lord. Yet Jesus forgave him—it was the first thing He did when He met him on Easter and said, "Peace be with you."

We will be judged by the same God-man who judged Simon Peter. We will be judged in the same way, too. We won't have to flinch in front of a harsh, unfeeling, perfection-demanding assessor of our flaws.

It would be good to put ourselves into the faulting and faltering heart of Simon Peter . . . and feel the Easter Peace of Christ who kindly passes judgment on our past:

Meditation:

In your imagination,
go to a small upper room.
It is dark;
the doors are locked. . . .

You are sad and afraid because of your past sins.
they have been sins of laziness.
You, too, have neglected to love,
as Simon Peter did when he fell asleep.
They have also been sins of weakness.
You, too, have impulsively denied your friendship with Christ,
as Simon Peter did
when he was afraid, in the courtyard of the High Priest.

Feel the guilt of these past failures—
feel the full weight of them. . . .

Feel how frightened you would be
if you were "put on the carpet"
and forced to explain your bad behavior
in front of a harsh demanding judge
(. . . someone like those people
who have shamed you in the past. . . .)

Then,
in this mood of apprehension,
let Jesus do what He did with Simon Peter:
let Him come through the locked doors of your fear. . . .

Let Him remind you—
gently, but very forcefully—
that He is your judge, nobody else.
Let Him forgive you
and give you His Easter message: "Peace be with you. . . ."

Let Him also tell you,
as He did Simon,
to forgive others
in the same way He has forgiven you. . . .

Then let Him start you off again on the right path,
suggesting how you should continue in His service. . . .

26
Jesus on Depending on Others' Opinions

Jesus said: "How can people like you believe, when you accept praise from one another yet do not seek the glory that comes from the One (God)?"

John 5:31-47

Reflection:

Today's Gospel gets to the root of the sin of the Pharisees. Pilate pronounced the sentence of crucifixion; but it was the Pharisees who handed Jesus over.

The ordinary people also were at fault. They were afraid of the power of the Pharisees. When the chips were down, when it came time to make a real stand "for or against," they said nothing to defend their popular hero—they just forgot their loyalty because they didn't want to start trouble for themselves. They may have *wished* Jesus were not so fiercely resented by the power structure of their time. But the fact is that He was . . . so the loud "Hosannas" of Palm Sunday became muffled as no one spoke well of Him.

One reason Jesus was so fiercely resented was jealousy. Mark's Gospel reports that Pilate knew the leaders brought Jesus to judgment "out of envy." (Mark 15, 6.) And what sparked this jealousy? Today's Gospel uncovers it: Jesus said to them, "How can you believe (in Me) when you seek praise from one another and not the praise that comes from God?"

This is, perhaps, the root-cause of sin in us all—seeking praise from others instead of from God. The Pharisees were concerned about their status and privileges. Jesus was taking this away with his emphasis on service rather than privileges. The people (like the parents of the man born blind, John 9) were concerned about "not getting kicked out of society"—"not making waves"—"not being with it." Simon Peter panicked on Good Friday morning, because he was made the butt of ridicule by soldiers and camp followers around a bonfire.

We often let ourselves become dejected or demoralized by similar pressures . . . or by simply not pleasing, or not helping, somebody we know.

When we do flounder in such a mood, we block the ability of grace to reach us—our attention (or aggravation) is centered on "seeking praise from other people, instead of working for the praise that comes from God."

Meditation:

In your imagination,
put on a doctor's outfit
and go to an X-ray room. . . .

Your "patient" is the sinful side of yourself:
sins of *offense*—hurting others,
                    or denying your friendship with Christ. . . .
or sins of *negligence*—like the ordinary people of Christ's time,
                    who would rather forget the whole thing
                    than risk disapproval
                    or financial disadvantage.

Examine these X-rays of your sinfulness.
Take a good look at them. . . .
Notice that the cause of your weakness
is *"seeking praise from others"*
(and getting discouraged when disapproval, or derision,
come your way.)

Make a further diagnosis:
What are your most serious needs to please?
Who are the people (or types of people)
who make you most anxious
when they threaten you with their displeasure?
Stay with the diagnosis as long as it
gives you wisdom
about the causes of your weakness. . . .

Then let Jesus come to help you with some remedies. . . .
As the Good Physician,
His opinion will be wise and kind.
He knows the best way to bring about a healing.
Listen to Him carefully. . . .

After He finishes—
as He is about to leave—
thank Him, in your own words,
for the grace—whatever grace—He gave you. . . .

27
Jesus—His Own Person

*Some of the people of Jerusalem remarked . . . "Still,
we know where this man is from. When the Messiah
comes, no one is supposed to know his origins." At
this, Jesus . . . cried out: "So you know me, and you
know my origins? The truth is, I have not come of myself. I was sent by One who has the right to send . . ."*

John 7:1-30

Reflection:

It is worthwhile, sometimes, to understand that early impres-
sions, learned in childhood, can put a kind of "fix" on later devel-
opment. For both good and ill, grownups have influenced, tremen-
dously, our opinions of ourselves. Whether they continue to deter-
mine our self-opinion is (or can be) within our own control.

Perhaps your early childhood was mostly a happy one—with
loving parents, accepting family, fine teachers, and good friends.
But there may have been a "clinker" or two among all these influ-
ential people. And all of them surely had their imperfections.

As a result, you may have been given "interpretations" about
how you would turn out—decisions about your ultimate worth—
judgments as to whether you were good or bad, capable or inadequate. These are like *tapes* played for you and put into your head·

"You won't accomplish much!"
"You're not as good as _____!"
"We, your childhood pals, prefer somebody else to
you!"
and so forth . . .

These negative tapes can keep playing all your life, and seriously demoralize you.

You are your own person, with responsibility for the *now* of
your life. You are not a predestined puppet, forced to live out
other people's *tape* of their forebodings about how poorly you
would probably end up.

Neighbors and the people of Jerusalem tried to "play tapes" on
Jesus: "We know where Jesus is from! He's just a small town boy
from Nazareth! He never will amount to much!"

Our Lord would not live out their tapes. We better not, either.

Meditation:

In your imagination,
go to a quiet library.
A soft rain is falling outdoors. . . .
you have the leisure
of an uninterrupted hour of an afternoon. . . .

Take yourself to a place
where cassettes may be played in privacy.
Replay—and relive—
some of the "negative tapes"
other people have made about you—
especially those interpretations of you
that, somehow, made you feel unlovable,
unwanted,
or inadequate. . . .

After you have heard all you can take of this,
stop the tapes,
rewind them,
and *PLAY OVER* them
by slowly reading today's Gospel out loud. . . .

Then rewind once more;
let Jesus come in
and play over the tapes again
by reminding you in His own words
how He is responsible for *your* origins:
He has created you,
He has died on the Cross for you,
and wants you to continue as His friend. . . .

When this is finished,
end by thanking Jesus
for the new tape He has personally recorded for you. . . .
Promise Him
that you will play it over, now and then
—especially when life seems so discouraging. . . .

28
Jesus on Being Rejected

The Pharisees retorted (to the temple guards), "You do not see any of the Sanhedrin believing in Jesus, do you? Or the Pharisees? Only (the people) who know nothing of the law. . . !" One of their own number, Nicodemus, spoke up to say, "Since when does our law condemn any man without first hearing him and knowing the facts?" They taunted him, "Do not tell us you are a Galilean, too . . ."

John 7:40-53

Reflection:

Just as it was true for Jesus in today's Gospel, so it is often true for us: there are some people—many people—who think well of us. We may not have touched them deeply, or for long . . . but we *have* touched them with our help, hospitality, or encouragement. Some of them admire us, speak well of us (as some did of Jesus); some of them speak ill of us or have totally forgotten us (as some did of our Lord, 20 centuries ago).

Then there is the same division among our closest friends. With our Lord, the odds were overwhelmingly against Him. Most of His own disciples left Him—60 out of 72—cf. John, Chapter 6. The great majority of the Scribes and Pharisees—those whom He tried hardest to reach—scorned Him and taunted Nicodemus for defending the prophet of Nazareth.

Jesus was left with only a handful who stayed true to Him: His mother and a few cousins (apparently, the rest of His kinsfolk had nothing to do with Him). Only 12 out of 72 disciples remained loyal and one of these 12 had already planned to betray Him. We can also assume there were no more than two of the religious leaders of the time, Nicodemus and Joseph of Arimethea, who defended Jesus.

One would call that a "bad field record" of popularity or appreciation. Perhaps we have a better record than our Master. Even so, there are some people who reject us outright . . . and even taunt those who stand by us.

For this reason, we must center within ourselves, make ourselves open to Christ's Spirit, and pray for the courage of our Lord. It is almost impossible, on our own, to keep our composure in the face of a betrayed trust, or a shattered hope. But we can do it if we allow Jesus to draw us into *His* composure . . . and this is what quiet prayer is all about:

Meditation:

In your imagination,
take yourself to a lonely island
off the rugged shore of the sea. . . .
You are wearing summer clothes and a thin windbreaker.
The wind is frightening;
the waves are fierce;
a terrible storm is coming. . . .

The roar and wind and wetness
represent all the people in your life
who have left you out in the cold,
and called you names,
and put you down,
and shattered your security
and even jeered at those who still remained your friends. . . .
You begin to feel lonely and frightened.
Stay with this feeling as long as you can stand it. . . .

When, in your imagination,
things seem to be as bad
as you have ever experienced them in reality,
relax . . . .
take your mind off your own troubles. . . .

Notice a large ship coming into sight.
It drops anchor not far away from you. . . .
Jesus is helmsman;
many of your good friends are with Him
you see them on deck, waving to you. . . .

Jesus leaves the ship,
walks on the water,
comes and takes you by the hand. . . .

The storm dies down.
Let yourself walk with Christ on top of the water. . . .
Then enter the ship.
He leads you to the comfortable, warm cabin. . . .

There Jesus and your friends enjoy your company,
in whatever way seems right to do so. . . .
(Notice, by the way,
how this experience is so good,
you easily forget the storm that came before it. . . .)

29
Jesus' Answer
to the Impatient

*The scribes and the Pharisees led a woman forward,
who had been caught in adultery. They made her stand
there in front of everyone. "Teacher," they said to
Jesus, "this woman has been caught in the act of adultery. In the law, Moses ordered such women to be
stoned. What do you have to say about the case?"...
Jesus simply bent down and started tracing on the
ground with his finger...*

John 8:1-11

Reflection:

For me, one of the most interesting aspects of this famous
episode in the Gospels, is the deliberate nonchalance of Jesus.

The story of our Lord's dealing with the Pharisees and the sinful
woman is best remembered for the mercy and patience of Jesus.
We identify with the sinner—if Jesus was so kind and protective of
her, against the fierce wrath of the "righteous ones," He will be
kind and gentle with us, too. A comforting thought ... and a true
one.

The story is also remembered for its "anti-hypocrisy campaign." Many people, immersed in their sinful ways, wear Christ's
words like a motto on their T-shirts ... as if to emblazon their bad
habits with justification from Jesus. "So what if I'm immoral, or
amoral! At least I'm not a hypocrite like those Pharisees of my
world who wish I'd change! Nobody's going to tell me what to do!
Didn't Jesus say 'Let him who is without sin cast the first stone' ?"

They blurt out such words of impudence ... and on they go,
reeling down the street, or raping, or robbing, or refusing to be
responsible—all the while thinking that Christ's words give them
safety from all censure.

The true way of understanding today's Gospel, is by identifying
with the sinful woman and praising God's mercy. The false way, is
by interpreting Christ's rebuke of the Pharisees as license for all to
do anything they please.

There is also another way to take in the meaning of this Gospel; identify with the Pharisees. How were they reacting? They were impatient for a fast answer from Jesus; and, even worse, they were rather angry with our Lord, wanting to pin Him down and make Him look foolish.

Sometimes we are like the Pharisees in this sense. We, too, get irritated at the way God permits evil to continue. We want to judge the sinners in no uncertain terms. We get upset by other people who are apparently heedless of how their selfishness is hurting others. We wonder—often, out loud—"How do they get away with it!" And we get terribly impatient with God when He permits all forms of human tragedy:

> "Why does God let drug-pushers live?"
> "Why does He allow the arsonist to burn poor people's homes?"
> "Why did He permit that drunken driver to maim my child?"

Like the Pharisees, we want to hurl an ultimatum at divinity, to put God on the witness stand—as though we were on an equal footing with Him (or, even worse, as though we were superior to His wisdom).

Such feelings do take over our judgment, now and then. It is part of our being upset at the time. They are not all that dangerous, or blasphemous, as long as we don't let indignation take control of us. Prayer is the best antidote for impudence—the prayer of a receiving heart, putting us in a ready mood for wisdom.

Meditation:

In your imagination,
go to a park within a big city.
You watch Jesus healing and helping others. . . .

In a vague way, this angers you:
You see other people's prayers answered,
and yours aren't.
This gets you thinking
about other times you have been dissatisfied with God
because of the evil that still exists in the world you know. . . .

You bring Jesus aside
and vehemently express your indignation
(let the words be as vehement as ever you have expressed them
to yourself or to someone else. . . .)

Jesus listens to you;
He lets you talk as long as you need to. . . .

Then watch,
as our Lord bends down
and begins to doodle,
nonchalantly,
in the dirt. . . .

Try to understand what Jesus means by what He draws. . . .
(The "doodles" may mean something; they may not. . . .)

Then you bend down
and draw your own "doodles" beside His. . . .
Look at what you've drawn
and wonder what the meaning of this is. . . .

Let Jesus explain why He drew as He did. . . .
Let Him also comment
(if He cares to)
about your drawing. . . .

Stay with His wisdom, here,
as long as it seems right to do so. . . .

30
Jesus and the
"Compulsive Do-Gooders"

Jesus said to the Pharisees: ". . . You belong to what is below; I belong to what is above. You belong to this world—a world which cannot hold me . . ."

John 8:21-30

Reflection:

Today's Gospel goes something like the outline of Robert L. Stevenson's novel, *Dr. Jekyll and Mr. Hyde.* The big difference is that Jesus is unlike the good doctor. He is *all* good—He is "from above." The Pharisees play the part of "Mr. Hyde"; they are the bad guys—they are "from below."

Of course, the Pharisees aren't *all* bad. They have some fine qualities. They are morally upright, for the most part; they are fierce advocates of God's honor; they are strong upholders of law and order. Their badness stems from an almost compulsive rigidity of role. They are so fixed in their desire to do good to others and give good advice to others (even to the point of telling God how He ought to run His world) that they are unable to be on the receiving end, unable to accept anything that does not come from their own initiative.

They don't want to understand that Jesus might be speaking the truth—a truth which they had not arrived at yet. They don't want to be in this inferior position, being students at the feet of a Master who tells them they must change their thinking and humbly accept advice.

They want to stay on top. They like their role of "master." They prefer to sway popular opinion until everybody's opinion becomes the one they already teach. It is their preference for dominant control that is bad. But from this, it all goes bad. They end by crucifying an innocent victim.

We have a danger of becoming "Mr. Hydes" to Jesus . . . unless, by prayer, we humbly take advice from Him and accept the faith in the way He gives it:

Meditation:

In your imagination,
go to a classroom, one that you remember. . . .

Pretend to be teacher for a while:
fill the classroom with all the people
you would like to give advice to—
especially those, this year,
whom you'd like to tell off. . . .
or tell them to "grow up!". . . .

Give them a good lecturing. . . .
Enjoy this pose for a while.
(It is the same activity, and posture of authority,
that the Pharisees enjoyed so much. . . .)

Now change roles. . . .
You become the student. . . .
(Let Jesus be in the back of the room, unnoticed.)

Get out a sheet of paper from the desk
and start taking dictation. . . .
You have a number of "teachers" up in front of the room.
They are some of the people
who, now and then, have given you advice.
Recall the criticisms and complaints against yourself
which you have received—especially most recently. . . .

Listen to them
in this "teacher to student" setting. . . .
In your imagination,
take down everything you hear. . . .

Then let Jesus come and stand beside you.
As He looks over your shoulder,
let Him weed out all the notes you took down. . . .
Let Him tell you,
with wisdom and gentleness,
which items of advice are "from above"
(therefore, to be followed);
and which items are "from below"
(therefore to be discarded). . . .

Remain with Jesus
as He adds some advice of His own. . . .
or else sums up what has already been expressed. . . .

31
Jesus on
Freedom and Slavery

Jesus said to those Jews who believed in him:
"If you live according to my teaching,
you are truly my disciples;
then you will know the truth,
and the truth will set you free."
"We are descendants of Abraham." was their answer.
"Never have we been slaves to anyone . . ."
Jesus answered them:
"I give you my assurance,
everyone who lives in sin
is the slave of sin . . ."   John 8:31-42

Reflection:

As Jesus speaks about slavery and freedom, there seems to be an obvious difference of opinion. Our Lord submits that the Pharisees are slaves. Their feathers are ruffled by that statement. "Nobody's pushing us around . . . we have never been slaves of any man!"

True enough. But they are slaves just the same—slaves to their own preconceived ideas. *They* are the teachers of law and order . . . *they* are the last word on good conduct and adequate expressions of religion. "Bossiness" is their problem. They are literally intractable—unable to be taught by Jesus, or by anyone.

Bossiness is one way to be enslaved. The positive side of "bossiness" is the desire to help and the capacity to lead. When we are in control of these qualities, we are doing well. We are in the driver's seat, harnessing our energies for good. But when the desire to influence others controls us, we become slaves of our own compulsion to be of help. Horse and rider change roles!

Three other "horses" fit this stagecoach—Time, Opinion, and Complacency. All of them are good servants—bad masters!

When we are in control of our life, "Time" is something we use productively; "Opinion" is a stimulus for us to be compassionately sensitive to other people's feelings; "Complacency" lets us enjoy life as it is and prudently realizes that we can't do everything all at once.

When we are *free*, we are like a driver handling all four horses and travelling well. When we are *slaves*, "Time" controls us (we are driven by its demands); or "Opinion" controls us (we get discouraged by somebody's disapproval, ready to sacrifice principles lest we upset anybody); or "complacency" sits in front of a TV set and controls us with inertia; or "bossiness" puts blinders on our eyes and a ring in our nose and we abjectly obey every whim of its demand that we always be helpful, always influencing others "for their own good."

The ideal is that these four powerful forces—Time, Compassion, Prudence (or Complacency) and Desire to Help—act *for* us. They are strong however; they are dangerously capable of suddenly enslaving us. In order to be powerful enough to control them, we must make ourselves available to the power of prayer.

Meditation:

In your imagination,
be the driver of a stagecoach,
masterfully guiding the horses mentioned above. . . .
Remember some times in your life
when you were in control;
enjoy the good feeling
that these experiences still can give you. . . .

Then stop and think
of your favorite way of letting yourself be enslaved
by Time, Opinion, Complacency or Bossiness. . . .

Let this "favorite way of being enslaved"
be identified as one of the horses. . . .
Then let this horse change places with you—
horse up on the driver's seat;
you down on the road,
harnessed and bridled,
whipped by your "master,"
and pulled by the other horses as well. . . .

Let this imaginative scene remind you
how, very often, in reality,
you do just that. . . .
Feel tired from it all
and disgusted with yourself. . . .

Then let Jesus ride up,
stop the coach,
harness the horse back where it belongs. . . .
and drive the team,
giving you advice as you ride along. . . .

32
Jesus on Death

*Jesus said . . . "I solemnly assure you, if a man is true
to my word he shall never see death."*

John 8:51-59

Reflection:

The "gathering storm" continues. As John remembers the events leading to the Passion of our Lord, the animosity of the Pharisees toward Jesus becomes more and more ominous. Jesus, forced so decisively to declare Himself, digs deeper and deeper into the most significant sign of Who He *is* and what He came for.

Our Lord wanted to make sure (so to speak) that His enemies would execute Him for the right reason. So, in order that there would be no doubt, Jesus hammered home the theme of death.

Death is the greatest proof of human limitation. Why continue to live, or to work, if we all will surely die . . . and then what will come of our labors?

The discouragement coming from this ultimate limitation is the basic cause for all other disillusionments as well. We can't be perfect . . . we can't please everybody . . . we can't be as good as _____, as successful as _____, and so on . . .

Because of the obvious limitation caused by death (and because of other limitations to our hopes caused by our mortal imperfections) the lives of all men, ultimately and fitfully, end up with a sigh: "Why try; who cares?"

Then Jesus came on earth to conquer this conclusive disillusionment. He lived a human life; and, as He lived, He knew that He would die. He would be as dead as any corpse.

But then He would be raised to life again. Death, as a finality, would not be experienced by Him. This was Jesus' most significant sign of who He is and what He promises. If we are true to His word, we shall never experience the finality of death.

Faith hears the same promise Jesus made 20 centuries ago. Prayer is the ear that hears it:

Meditation:

In your imagination,
return to the cemetery
where you once buried the body of someone you loved. . . .

Remember when the loved one was alive,
full of plans
and enthusiasm
and goodness. . . .

Then remember this dear one dead. . . .
Think of the person as "just dead":
consider how futile all the life was,
if this was how it ended. . . .

From these somber thoughts,
consider how futile *your* life is,
since you, too, must die
and rest in dirt. . . .

Remaining in the cemetery, beside the grave,
let your imagination feel the sun come out
and warm your shoulders. . . .
Let the words of today's Gospel reach your heart. . . .
Feel the power of Christ's resurrection;
sense the energy of Him, coming out of the grave
to live more fully and more richly than before.

He *did it!*
The person you are thinking about in the cemetery
will also do it, thanks to Jesus;
so will you. . . .

Stay with these comforting thoughts,
warmed by the rays of the sun,
as long as it seems helpful to you. . . .

33
Jesus on Self-Awareness

When the Jews reached for rocks to stone him, Jesus protested to them, "Many good deeds have I shown you from the Father. For which of these do you stone me?" The Jews retorted, "It is not for any 'good deed' that we are stoning you, but for blaspheming. You who are only a man are making yourself God."

John 10:31-42

Reflection:

In the last analysis, it was Jesus' "claim of consciousness," not His "expressions of behavior" that caused His crucifixion.

Jesus forced His enemies to admit this much, anyway! "I have done many good works among you—for which of these do you wish to stone me?" They snapped back: "Not for any of your good works (which they publicly acknowledged were good—) but for claiming you are the only Son of God."

At least this nailed it down. It was our Lord's awareness of who He was and why He was doing His good works—this was precisely what got Him into trouble with the authorities.

Here, in today's Gospel, the superiority of a person's inner faculties of mind and will is understood to be superior to the outer qualities of behavior and activity. Admittedly, it is hard to separate inner feelings from outward behavior. Ordinarily, what we *think* about ourselves will be expressed by what we *do*. In a certain sense, it is true that "deeds speak louder than words." A hypocrite can talk about noble goals; but people will laugh at his pretensions if he does not live up to them.

But only in a *certain* sense do deeds speak louder. In another sense, it is the other way around. Surely, it was Jesus' *words*, His "claim of consciousness," that spoke louder to the Pharisees. Christ's deeds were approved of; but the awareness of *why* He did what He did was the cause of their reproach.

Jesus not only proved a point here, He preached a point as well. It is not enough that we be good people—kind, considerate, accommodating. We must know *why* we do so. We must know who we are when we do good. We must strengthen our inner faculties of mind and will—not going through life instinctively, like animals, but consciously aware of our God-given reasons for living this way:

Meditation:

In your imagination,
go to a quiet place—
the first quiet place that comes easily to mind. . . .

Be alone,
long enough to slow thoughts down. . . .
Just be there
with that kind of peace you had, in the same place,
once before. . . .

Let two or three people visit you—
people who,
for one reason or another,
admire you.
They have already thanked you;
they have praised you for some kindness you did for them.

Let them thank you the same way now
with as much as you can remember
of the same words and the same smiles. . . .

Now let Jesus join your group.
Let Him ask you what you've been talking about. . . .
You tell Him. . . .
(Don't be embarrassed;
don't try to be a "phoney" with false humility—
you are simply reporting
the words of gratitude
that other people have expressed. . . .)

Let our Lord relax
after He hears your report.
Give Him time to enjoy it. . . .

Then let Him suggest to you
how you could have been even *better*
in doing those acts of kindness
if you were more aware of why you were doing it
and more aware of how grace was helping you through it all. . . .

And let Him gently urge you
(in His own way)
to be more alive to your link with Him—
as the good you do
is even more consciously filled with meaning. . . .
and even more graciously done with joy. . . .

34
Jesus on Laziness

*The chief priests and the Pharisees called a meeting of
the Sanhedrin. "What are we to do," they said, "with
this man performing all sorts of signs? If we let him go
on like this, the whole world will believe in him. Then
the Romans will come in and sweep away our sanctu-
ary and our nation."*

John 11:45-57

Reflection:

There is a certain "inertia of initiative" that gets to everybody,
draining away life's energies and enthusiasm. Call it by different
names: "stand-pat-ism," "don't-make-waves-ism," "I'm-too-
tired-to-think-about-it-now-ism" . . . whatever.

There is a part of all of us that is reluctant to begin a new thing,
hesitant to change, unwilling to start the engines of the soul. Such
an attitude describes young teenagers at an informal dance: boys
in one corner, girls in another—nobody moving. It describes many
people who want to pray but are too lazy to get out of the chair. It
often describes those who make a weekend retreat and want to see
improvement in their lives, but naively think that happiness can
happen without personal hard work. It describes some members of
a family who realize there is a problem, but—"head in the sand"
fashion—think that the problem will go away if nobody brings it
up.

It also describes the Pharisees in today's Gospel: "If we let
Jesus of Nazareth continue, we will have to change our attitude . . .
we won't have the prominent places in our nation (and all the security and fringe-benefits that go with it). Caesar will wonder
what's up and take away the status quo!"

The inertia of the Pharisees led to the murder of an innocent
victim. Our inertia may not have such dramatic consequences. But
it does—always—have deadening consequences to some degree.
We make "bad news" for ourselves and others whenever we prefer
to continue our unhappy "half alive" lives just because we are
used to it and do not want to change.

It is this cancer of the soul that Jesus addresses in the Gospel
just before Holy Week. Will laziness let Jesus die to us?

Meditation:

In your imagination,
take yourself to an overstuffed chair,
in a smoke-filled uncomfortable room. . . .
Put your legs up
and cover yourself with a blanket that reads: "Yes, BUT . . ."

Then let friends come into your room
and present you with challenges—
challenges to grow,
to do more with your life,
to develop virtues more solidly
or get rid of bad habits more determinedly. . . .

Reply to them:
(as you often have, in real life)
"Yes, BUT . . . I'm too tired . . .
                    I might lose out on what I have . . .
                    It's too much trouble . . .
                    I don't want to make waves . . ."

Then let Jesus enter the room,
open the windows to clear the air. . . .
and
'nduce you to begin—
to get up from the chair and start moving—
little by little—
one practical step at a time. . . .

After the suggestions,
after you've given time to let the words sink in,
thank Jesus
and say goodbye
in whatever way seems right to both of you. . . .

Finally, turn to your friends
(they have listened in on the whole thing)
and repeat to them
what you remember Jesus having said to you. . . .

Ask them if you understood Him properly . . .
and ask them if they have any further suggestions
about how to put our Lord's advice into action. . . .

35
Jesus on Good Influences in Our Lives

The great crowd . . . came out, not only because of Jesus but also to see Lazarus, whom he had raised from the dead. The fact was, the chief priests planned to kill Lazarus too, because many Jews were going over to Jesus and believing in him on account of Lazarus.

John 12:1-11

Reflection:

Most people do not think often enough, or long enough, about the influence of LADNACS in their life. LADNACS is SCANDAL, spelled backward. One is the contrast of the other; LADNACS stands for just the opposite of all the ideas and feelings that the word SCANDAL brings to mind.

Scandal we know about. We know its power to harm, its demoralizing effects, its way of poisoning cooperation and trust. We spend a lot of time thinking about the "bad apples" in the bushel. We use up a lot of energy being indignant about certain notorious blights on family, church or community.

It is proper, of course, to be upset by scandal. We should do something about it when we can. But LADNACS is just as power-ful an influence in the world—and this is a positive and productive influence. A person who is a *good* example—a "good apple"— sets a wave of goodness in motion. Often, though, by not thinking of this, we tend to weaken the force of it.

The LADNACS I speak of are not only found among people who do good, conducting themselves with exemplary helpfulness. LAD-NACS are also found among people who let themselves *be* helped. We are inspired by the good that happened to them and want some of it ourselves:

> "If that married couple got help to save their marriage, so can I."
> "If so-&-so found a way to stop over-eating or smoking or drinking, so can I."
> "If the retreat, or prayer-meeting, did so much good for my friends, maybe I should try it too."

Today's Gospel documents a beautiful "LADNACS-influence" that Lazarus had on his friends and neighbors. "A great crowd

came also to see Lazarus whom Jesus had raised from the dead . . .
indeed, it was *on his account* that many were going over to Jesus."

Lazarus had great influence simply by letting himself be known
as somebody whom Jesus had raised to life and health. It would be
good to think more, and prayerfully, about the powerful influences
that have blessed our lives:

Meditation:

In your imagination,
go to a busy airport. . . .
Prepare to meet a plane coming in.
It is called the "LADNACS SPECIAL"

The plane arrives with a number of people,
young and old,
all of whom have been "Lazaruses" for you. . . .
One way or another,
they have influenced you for good:
they encouraged you;
they gave you confidence;
they somehow renewed, "resurrected," hope in yourself,
and in others,
and in God,
when you were discouraged. . . .

Meet them as they come through the gate.
Introduce each one to the others. . . .
(It may be the first time many of them have ever met.)
Take all the time that is needed for this. . . .

Then invite them all to dinner.
You have a dining room prepared,
in a quiet place. . . .
Share good times again. . . .

After dinner,
let some of them speak,
in their own words,
about the good things God has done for them;
let them bear witness
to the way grace worked in their lives. . . .

Finally, let someone
(whichever person seems to be the right one)
end the evening
with a prayer of gratitude to Jesus. . . .

36
Jesus on Discouragement

Jesus, reclining with his disciples, grew deeply troubled. He went on to give this testimony:
"I tell you solemnly,
one of you will betray me."
... He dipped the morsel of food, then took it and gave it to Judas, son of Simon Iscariot ... No sooner had Judas eaten the morsel than he went out. It was night.

John 13:21-38

Reflection:

There is one aspect of prayer which is probably the most important for helping us ordinary mortals stay healthy, both spiritually and psychologically. Discouragement is our greatest sickness. It is the source of enervation, anger, jealousy, and a whole smorgasbord of "mini-suicides" (drugs, drink, overeating, workaholism, televisionitis, pouting, etc.).

Prayer is needed to unlock ourselves from these deadening surrenders. The type of prayer that can do this for us is "Master/disciple meditation." We must take the time and effort needed to penetrate the Scriptures and observe closely what actually did happen to Jesus—how He operated within the moods, events, challenges and disappointments that came His way. Then, "since the disciple cannot expect to be greater than the Master," it won't surprise us when the same things come our way.

By meditating on Jesus as Master to us disciples, we will not only be saved from the querulous "why-does-this-have-to-happen-to-me" complaint ... we will also have the promised strength to keep going despite our disappointments. As God gave His own Son strength to continue, so does He give us the very same.

One disappointment—and perhaps the hardest one to suffer—is the hurt of not being able to help someone close. Parents, at times, are powerless to do anything as they watch their grownup son or daughter reject every value of their upbringing. A friend finds it impossible to help the madness in another. A coach or priest or teacher sees a youngster throw away his gifts for a choice that will ruin him. And those who care must stay on the sidelines—as Jesus did with Judas Iscariot—and let it happen.

Our Lord was saddened by the unreachableness of Judas; we, too, have every right to be saddened when something similar happens to us. But our Lord did not give up on the rest of His disciples

simply because He failed to communicate with one of them—He
kept going; we had better not give up on the rest of the people in
our lives, either. In order to keep going under circumstances which
are causing a deeply troubled mood in us we need help. We need
the Spirit of Jesus Christ . . . we need to pray:

Meditation:

In your imagination,
go to the garden of a private home. . . .

People are having a picnic there (already begun);
you have been invited.
There are ten or so people—
all of them close friends of yours.
One of them is a person you have tried to help,
but to no avail. . . .

Let yourself feel the disappointment of your helplessness. . . .
link your feeling
with Christ's own sadness over Judas' "inaccessibility". . . .

Give this person the choicest morsel of your food;
then let the person leave your company. . . .
Feel the "jolt" of his/her leaving. . . .

Entrust the person to God
—and to the chance that someone else,
    somewhere,
    sometime,
    will finally be of help. . . .

Then look around you:
to the rest of the company
—to the friends and family that you still do have
—and keep going. . . .
Don't give up
because there is one less person around the picnic table. . . .

Let Jesus, who is your Host
(in whose garden you are relaxing)
ask for silence
and gently offer suggestions
on how you can continue,
even in your sadness over a lost friend. . . .

37
Jesus on Hospitality

The disciples came up to Jesus and said, "Where do you wish us to prepare the Passover supper for you?" He said, "Go to this man in the city and tell him, 'The Teacher says, My appointed time draws near. I am to celebrate the Passover with my disciples in your house.' "

Matt. 26:14-25

Reflection:

Usually, it is a hard thing to be "just an onlooker—in the wings" when important doings or interesting conversations are going on around you, but without you.

This seemed to be the case of the man in today's Gospel. Jesus must have talked to him beforehand. He must have been a man of some means—wealthy enough to provide cooks and service and a private room capable of handling a leisurely supper for 13 people.

Who was he? What happened to him later? Where did he stay while Jesus and the disciples were eating their Passover meal and receiving their first holy communion and when all but one of them were ordained as priest?

We don't know. If I were the man in question (who obviously loved Jesus enough to be a very gracious host) I would have wanted to "be in on the action" . . . to know what was going on . . . to be a vital part of it.

It seems he wasn't. My guess is that he was a kind of "bouncer," protecting the entrance to make sure unwelcome guests didn't crash the party.

Everyone of us takes this role on occasion. We are a "third party" setting up a meeting for two other people to establish firmer grounds of friendship, or to effect a reconciliation. We introduce a loved one to someone else, who introduces our loved one to a new life or a lucky break or a promotion involving responsibilities that have nothing to do with us. And we are left "holding the bag" (or the check) and wishing we could be more involved, but having little control over it.

Sometimes it is good to identify with the "unnamed people" in the Gospel—praying to Jesus in this role. Prayer can make the hard times in our lives easier.

Meditation:

In your imagination,
go to the stairway of a large room
and sit on the bottom step,
elbows on knees, head in your hands. . . .

It is quiet where you are;
but in one of the upstairs rooms
there is activity. . . .
Imagine the activity
to be a "re-run" of something that has happened in your real life
when you were a "third party" as suggested above. . . .

As you are brooding,
let two people come into your solitude:
Jesus
and the man who provided for the Last Supper. . . .

After you greet them both,
let the man tell you how he felt
when he was excluded as you are. . . .

Let both Jesus and His friend
share their original conversation,
months before,
when they planned the Supper. . . .
Let Jesus retell the reasons
why He wanted privacy with His disciples
and why He asked for hospitality from this particular person. . . .

Listen
as Jesus praises him for his self-sacrificing goodness. . . .
Then let Jesus praise you
for the same
in your life. . . .

Finally, it may be that our Lord
can foresee more opportunities for you
to be a humble agent of reconciliation in behalf of others. . . .
Of course, He can foresee them;
perhaps He would like to tell you about them.
If so, let Him speak to you. . . .

38
Jesus—Healing the Way He Wants To

Jesus had loved his own in this world, and he would show his love for them to the end . . . He picked up a towel and tied it around himself. Then he poured water into a basin and began to wash his disciples' feet and dry them with the towel . . . Thus he came to Simon Peter, who said to him, "Lord, are you going to wash my feet?" . . . "You shall never wash my feet!" Jesus answered, "If I do not wash you, you will have no share in my heritage." "Lord," Simon Peter said to him, "then not only my feet, but my hands and head as well."

John 13:1-15

Reflection:

We know about Simon Peter's triple denial of our Lord, late Holy Thursday night. We also know how he fell asleep, three times, when Jesus begged him to stay awake during the long evening hours of our Lord's distress.

There is another three-fold mistake he made, even earlier that night. He made three *exaggerated responses* to Christ's request. It is not that Peter was malicious, or that his behavior was evil. It's just that his impetuosity kept missing the mark. He blunted the message his Master was trying to convey.

Twice, Jesus tried to wash Simon Peter's feet. Twice the Apostle begged off. He meant well, but . . . *First*, (as so often happens with good people who feel compelled to be on the giving end of all giving-receiving relationships,) Simon Peter refused to let Jesus do such a menial act of service for him.

His refusal was refused. Jesus severely warned him: "If you don't let Me love you, *My* way, you will have to part company with Me." So . . . *Second,* (as so often happens with us all,) Simon Peter went to the other extreme. His words could be understood as meaning: "Wash everything! Don't just stop with one thing—fix me over completely . . . I'm so bad a sinner, stop at nothing!"

We have experienced impulsiveness like Peter's. Jesus wants to heal us; but our "all or nothing" instinct either won't let God do anything for us, or else He has to do it *all* Himself, do us over completely!

Jesus stood His Ground with Simon Peter. He still insisted that all He wanted to do—and *what* He wanted to do—was to wash the man's *feet.* Then (as I interpret it) Peter tried a *Third Dodge:* "Not my feet—wash my hands and head instead! (or at least, concentrate more on my hands and head than on what *You* mentioned!) These are the things *I* have decided need it more. Anyway, it's neater to work on these parts of my body than on the feet, which are embarrassing to me."

Simon Peter speaks like so many of us. Jesus has a certain thing to help us with—a certain challenge to grow—a certain "call to change" that we honestly and resolutely have to face . . . but we prefer to concentrate on something else because the "something else" is less embarrassing or less demanding.

With Peter's insight (which he learned the hard way) let us pray.

Meditation:

In your imagination,
go to the side altar

of a church that you remember with good memories. . . .
It is the evening of Holy Thursday.
The Blessed Sacrament is honored on the altar. . . .
Candles and flowers surround our Lord with silent praise. . . .

Remain there, in prayer,
as long as possible. . . .
Let Jesus love you. . . .
(Even if you feel uncomfortable by this love,
or feel unworthy of it,
do not resist it. . . .)

Let Him touch—and cleanse—
that part of you
that *He* wants to. . . .
Don't divert Him
with demands that He "do everything"
or with any changing of the subject on your part. . . .

Do not speak. . . .
Do not talk about other problems you may have,
or other things
that *you* think need attention more. . . .

Just be conscious of His healing power. . . .
and of His love
and nourishment. . . .
which He is pleased to give you—*His* way. . . .

39
Jesus the Consoler

Near the cross of Jesus there stood his mother . . .
Seeing his mother there with the disciple whom he
loved, Jesus said to his mother, "Woman, there is your
son." In turn he said to the disciple, "There is your
mother." From that hour onward, the disciple took her
into his care.

John 18:1-19, 42

Reflection:

Good Friday is good in so many ways, it would be foolhardy to
even try to be comprehensive. Let me, instead, suggest just one of
many possible approaches for meditating on this inexhaustible
scene.

Let me select the brief interchange between Jesus, Mary and the
disciple whom Jesus loved: "Woman," our Lord said in His last
hour, "behold your son (take care of all the sons and daughters
that you shall mother for all time). Then, turning to His disciple,
"Behold your mother (take care of her").

Even in His anguish, Jesus proved Himself to be a thoughtful
son. He made sure that all His Church would never lack a Mother
to trust in and to be comfortable with. He also made sure that
Mary would be provided for—she would be protected from human
vultures who preyed on helpless widows.

Surely, this last communication of our Lord before He gave up
His spirit has profound significance. Prayerful people, from the
early Church Fathers to modern Scripture scholars, continue to
draw rich theological meaning from these words. Here, we are not
concerned with these deeper understandings. We are reflecting
only on the lesson implied by the most ordinary and obvious understanding of what went on.

I take it (pardon my boldness, Lord) to be the greatest sign of
maturity when a person, in his sadness, is concerned about others
. . . and not simply locked into his own grief.

Some people, more selfish than Jesus, walk with "blinders of
self-pity" when faced with overwhelming sadness or helplessness.
They cannot get over it! Suddenly, the people around them do not

exist. The more that pain becomes unbearable, the more does hope become unmentionable—life shrivels up and it is of no concern that friends or family still have a right to be loved.

Other people accept their "Calvary-like" situation with more of the wide-eyed carefulness of Christ. They suffer just as much, but much more selflessly. They refuse to run away from life. They refuse to escape from grief by giving in to self-pity. They, like Jesus, remember others even as they are stricken down by loss or loneliness or pain of death. Let us pray for the grace to do the same.

Meditation:

In your imagination,
go to a windy hill—
you are alone. . . .

The hill is unprotected,
the scenery is severe, foreboding. . . .
the clothes you wear are not enough
to keep away the bite of wind. . . .

Let the harshness of it
be as much as you can bear. . . .
then let it be a little more. . . .

On this unprotected hill,
think of your favorite temptation to give up,
or to get "down" on life. . . .
(Everyone has a certain pattern
of arriving at such feelings of destruction or self-pity.
Try to discover yours. . . .)

Remember a recent time when you felt grief
because of these feelings,
or because of a death of a loved-one,

or because of physical pain,
or anxiety,
or a frustration in life,
whatever. . . .

Feel, once again.
the urge to "put blinders on" —
to settle down in your own sadness. . . .
Be oblivious, once more,
to life around you. . . .
Feel, once again,
so sad that it is almost too much to bear. . . .
then feel it even worse. . . .

When it becomes unbearable,
relax. . . .
Let Mary put her hand on your shoulder.
She is the Mother of Jesus;
thanks to Good Friday, she is now your Mother, too.
Spend some time, on that fierce hill,
simply being aware of her presence. . . .

She knows what she is doing. . . .
she knows she has the power from God to do it:
she gently pulls away the blinders from your eyes. . . .

She shows you the other people in your life. . . .
People who need your care
and the hospitality of your attention —
people who rely on you
as John relied on Mary;
as Mary relied on John. . . .

Let her counsel you. . . .
let her show you how
to live with grief
on your long, Good Friday afternoons. . . .

40
Jesus—Waiting for Easter

The First Reading:
From the Book of Exodus 14:15-15,1

When Israel saw . . . the great power that the Lord had
shown against the Egyptians, they feared the Lord and
believed in him . . .

The Second Reading
From the Book of Isaias 54:5-14

With enduring love I take pity on you,
    says the Lord, your redeemer.
This is for me like the days of Noah,
    when I swore that the waters of Noah
    should never again deluge the earth;
So I have sworn not to be angry with you,
    or to rebuke you.
Though the mountains leave their place
    and the hills be shaken,
My love shall never leave you . . .

The Third Reading:
From the Gospels of Matthew 28:1-10
Mark 16:1-8
Luke 24:1-12

On the first day of the week, at dawn, the women came
to the tomb bringing the spices they had prepared . . .
When they looked they found that the stone had been
rolled back. (It was a huge one.) . . .
. . . When they entered the tomb, they did not find the
body of the Lord Jesus. While they were still at a loss
what to think of this, two men in dazzling garments
appeared beside them. Terrified, the women bowed to

the ground. The men said to them, "Why do you search for the living One among the dead? He is not here; he has been raised up . . ."
They hurried away from the tomb half-overjoyed, half-fearful, and ran to carry the good news to his disciples . . .
The story seemed like nonsense (to the apostles) and they refused to believe them.
Peter, however, got up and ran to the tomb. He stooped down but could see nothing but the wrappings. So he went away full of amazement at what had occurred.

Reflection:

The last of the meditations is exceptional. It is longer than the others; and it reflects on Scripture readings of the Old Testament as well as the Gospel.

It is somehow fitting that it should be different. Of all the meditations, the one that most easily fits our kind of "guided imagery prayer" is the Easter Saturday Night Vigil that waits for the Risen Savior.

The mood is one of passive anticipation. As we wait, we wonder about the way Christ conquered death for all of us. Along with death, He conquered all of death's "attendant sicknesses," as well. We wonder how He did it; we watch with the eyes of faith.

The Church gives us a choice of readings to help us wait the night out—helping us reflect on how God, so often in history, intervened with His merciful assistance.

Besides the Gospel, we need to consider the 3rd and 4th readings. The 3rd is the one "must" for this night's Liturgy of the Word—the passage from Exodus that reveals how God sent Moses to lead His people out of bondage.

Another choice is the next reading, from Isaias—how God encouraged His people by reminding them of the covenant already made in Noah's time.

As we wait for the brightness of the "Eastering" of Jesus, we wait with a blend of feelings and moods very much like those experienced by the first disciples. We, too, have a strange mixture of both hope in Christ and worry about ourselves—both confidence and fearfulness—both faith and self-fixations.

Let us pray, not with simplicity (we are not that simple). Let us pray with the admitted honesty of our very complex hearts:

Meditation on the First Reading:

In your imagination,
go into the airless, lifeless tomb
where the dead corpse of Jesus is lying. . . .

Be a part of Him, somehow—
a part of His death. . . .

Then experience—inside Him—
the moment, in the stillness of the night,
when He is lifted up by His Father,
freed from the shroud that bound Him,
whisked away from the airless tomb,
and
placed free
and full of life
on top of the same hill
which so recently was the altar of His death. . . .

Continue to be with Him—inside Him—
as His human mind collects His thoughts. . . .
as He realizes how this night
is so, so different
from any other time that He woke up from sleep. . . .

A scene comes to Him
—and to you, since you are within Him—
about the Prophet Moses who preceded Him. . . .
Moses was given power by God
to go into Egypt
and lead the people out of slavery into freedom.
Moses did just that.
God protected His people
from being drowned in the impassible sea. . . .
After all were safe,
on the other side,
Moses climbed a hill

and saw angry mercenaries,
armed to the teeth,
pursuing their slaves to force them back into bondage. . . .
The sea engulfed God's enemies.
Moses breathed easily,
rejoiced in the security of his new life
—on the other side of the sea—
and praised God for the power of His faithfulness. . . .

Great as this was,
it was only a pale hint
of what the Risen Christ experienced. . . .

Jesus, too, breathed easily.
He passed over the sea of Death.
He is forever secure in His new Life. . . .
He is the God-man, loving His Father perfectly,
forever. . . .

He is the path for all God's chosen people—
the way for all of us to escape the land of bondage
and the puppet-chains of mercenaries
and the fear of death. . . .
and all life's "little deaths". . . .

Be with Jesus
as He praises God His Father. . . .

He remembers
on His hill on the other side of the sea of Death,
what He went through,
trustingly,
for love of us. . . .

Now He is full of life,
more abundant even than before,
thanking God with wonder and with praise. . . .

Be with Jesus in His prayer;
just be with Him. . . .

Meditation on the Second Reading:

In your imagination,
(after the reading of Isaias 54),
go off, by yourself, to a lovely meadow. . . .

Be a youth again,
in the best memories you have of yourself. . . .
Lie down on the grass.
It is a sunny afternoon.
There is a large tree on the top of the hill.
Enjoy this, too. . . .

As you are there,
remember the wonderful ideals you had when you were young
—how good life might be for you. . . .
—what beautiful things you might do. . . .
(The rosiest of prospects,
the happiest of hopes,
you ever had. . . .
Remember these again. . . .)

Then let life continue. . . .
In your memory,
recall the coming of bitterness and cynicism,
hurts and disappointments. . . .
Recall your own sins and mistakes
and the rueful sadness still attending them. . . .
Recall the march of age,
the slowing-down of energy,
the missed opportunities,
the rejection of friends,
the ending of past joys. . . .
Recall, too,
whatever in your present life
fills you with anxiety and dread
with a fixation on fear
               or on a certain sense of failure. . . .

Let all these sombre, anxious thoughts
ruin your composure in the meadow. . . .

Let them seem to you
like a fast-moving, frightening, engulfing flood. . . .
Already this sea of restlessness
is rising over your shoes,
then up to your knees. . . .
then on and on and on. . . .
until you wonder how long it will be
before you drown. . . .

Clouds are bending
with more and more outbursts of anxieties. . . .
All alone, there, you are helpless. . . .
(As was Noah and his family
and all the people who lived in Noah's time. . . .)

As you are about to despair,
look over your shoulder. . . .
Beyond the tree,
on the top of the meadow,
Mary appears to your vision—
Mary is on one side;
St. Joseph is on the other. . . .
They smile assuringly;
and put a finger over their lips to warn you to be silent. . . .

Mary then calls to some friends of yours—
people who have helped you in the past. . . .
Joseph calls to some of your friends
who have already died. . . .
With Mary and Joseph giving instructions,
your friends get to work
to build you an ark
(or boat, or ship, or raft—
whatever kind of vessel seems right for you. . . .)
They enjoy their work,

joking with each other
as they cooperate
to build a seaworthy craft for you
so that you may ride out the storms of failure and anxiety. . . .

Get on board. . . .
Find a comfortable spot. . . .
Feel the safety and security
of friends and saints like Mary and Joseph helping you. . . .
Stay with this feeling of safety-within-storm
as long as it seems good and profitable. . . .

Then notice
that the rain has subsided. . . .
The flood of fears and tears drains off. . . .
and you are settled,
once again,
in your now dry meadow, beside the tree. . . .

You notice another hill
—over and up from yours.
It is Calvary. . . .
Jesus has been there for some time,
still musing on the full meaning of His Resurrection. . . .

He waves to you,
calls you to come over. . . .
You go. . . .

Our Lord helps you to understand
that if Isaias could encourage the Chosen People
by referring to God's saving power in the past
(in Noah's time)
all the more so
can you have reason for trust in the Father's mercy—
a greater than Noah is here!

Then feel the sun break through the clouds. . . .

Stand in awe
as you see the most brilliant rainbow develop
before your eyes. . . .

As you watch,
let Jesus speak to you
of the meaning of the rainbow and of His Resurrection. . . .
how,
thanks to God's "keeping care,"
you never,
never,
need to fear the flood. . . .

Meditation on the Third Reading—

In your imagination,
find yourself in an upper room,
just as a group of women burst in,
with bewildered and bewildering excitement. . . .

They have just seen the empty tomb of Jesus.
They noticed the linens laid neatly on the cot of stone;
they heard some wild stories
about His being risen from the dead
and gone to Galilee, or someplace. . . .
Every one of them seems to have a different story,
and each spills over into other news,
and none of it makes much sense. . . .

The Apostles, too,
(some of them)
have news about things happening unexpectedly. . . .

Be with their confusion
and mix your own with theirs. . . .

Remain with them:
waiting. . . .

waiting. . . .
waiting. . . .

They have faith in Jesus,
but not very much of it.
They listen as you tell your story:
how you, too, have faith in Jesus,
but not very much of it:

> You, too, are depressed, at times;
> and often quite confused.
> You, also, have had ideals
> which have been, now and then, shot down
> (like the hopes the disciples had
> before Good Friday crushed them).
> You also
> (like the disciples, early Easter morning)
> have had the reverse of the above experience—
> just when you were getting used to being crushed,
> you suddenly sensed God's powerful resurging strength,
> somehow,
> within you.
> This new-found "half joy" feeling
> came to you as hints,
> intimations,
> garbled stories about how other people
> experienced the Lord.
> You half-believed this new "Good News"
> and, as you did,
> the mood of cynicism and surrender
> which you were buried in
> was rolled away.

They know how you feel—
the other disciples in that upper room. . . .
They feel it too.
Let them share their stories. . . .

Then, unexpectedly,
Mary returns. . . .

She was out somewhere.
Her face is radiant. . . .
No one could possibly not-love her at this moment. . . .

Everyone quiets down. . . .
There is a curious expectancy in the air. . . .
Mary speaks of her private conversation
she just had
with her Risen Son. . . .

"Yes, risen!
"No more to fear. . . .
"He will see you all soon. . . .
"Be patient. . . .
"Watch and wait. . . . and pray. . . ."

Then Mary explains
that there are some things Mother and Son shared
that can't be talked about.
But some of it she can share;
and so she does. . . .

Listen,
as you wait in the upper room,
with a mixture of both
    faith in God and fear of self;
    enjoyment of Christ's love and puzzlement over His doings;
    saintliness and sinfulness;
    trust and impatient irritations. . . .

You wait,
as the women and the disciples wait,
with all this "mix" inside you. . . .

And Mary speaks of the peace that is hers. . . .

And Mary helps you with your waiting,
with words that only she can say,
from Christ. . . .
which are only meant for you. . . .
in prayer. . . .

Appendix 1: Some Further Notes on Memory and Imagination and Their Influences on Prayer.

"You must be self-controlled and alert to be able to pray."
(1 Peter 4, 7—Good News Translation)

Prayer is not all that easy for the average person. Thoughts about past events crowd in to the time. Concerns about the future do the same.

Most people want to pray. As mentioned in the Introduction, most people feel good when they take the time, as Jesus did, to "go away to a quiet place" in order to praise God and thank Him and ask for help.

We *like* to pray . . . BUT: our past and our future, bullied by memory and imagination, crowd in to our present time and cause distraction. It is difficult to pray because it is difficult to live in the *present.*

You know what I mean. Doubtless, you have your own story to tell; yet, it would be something like these three examples. Three people dropped into church, one afternoon. Each tried to pray, but each struggled painfully. Here are their stories:

Story One:

Tom was coming home from high school. Busy day. Many things went right; *But* he got yelled at by one of his teachers when it wasn't his fault . . . he got a "put down" by somebody he thought was his friend . . . he made a stupid mistake in the math exam . . . a girl he admired gave him the cold shoulder.

His memory would not let go. Those hurts were like a sore tooth he just couldn't leave alone. Then, as if all this wasn't bad enough, his imagination was running him ragged: how would he greet his friend tomorrow . . . how would he react to that teacher from now on . . . would that math mistake give him an "F" and how would he explain *that* to his parents . . . would he just quit trying to interest that girl; or what would he do . . .

So Tom really was not at prayer at all. He was not praying because he was not present to his time of praying. Mind and heart and feelings were pulled in various directions—pulling him away from prayer. Memory was putting him back in school, playing reruns of the difficult events of the day. Imagination was placing him into the future—tomorrow's school-day or next week's report card showdown.

Memory and imagination have a way of playing the same tricks on us if we don't do something about it.

Story Two:

Ellen is a wife and the mother of four children who range from college to grammar school. She finished her shopping and made a visit on the way home. She really wanted to pray, but . . . a number of other things went wrong for her during that day (her hurts, similar to the ones Tom couldn't stop recalling). Besides these, she also hurt from memories that went further back . . . and deeper down. It seems that, every time she paused to pray, the insult of her best friend came back to haunt her . . . or it was the malicious gossip of that neighbor who told lies about her children . . . or the inconsiderateness of other members of her family who were too busy to do their share of caring for mother . . . or the dull pain about husband, not nearly as thoughtful as he used to be . . .

Added to hurts coming from the memory, imagination played its havoc, too. When Ellen looked into the future, she saw possibilities, all right—but possibilities of disaster: "Will the oldest son ever find himself?" "Will our marriage get worse and worse?" "What have I done wrong in bringing up the twins, and how will it affect their future?" "Why don't I have the pep and the patience I used to have—and is this going to get worse?"

The thoughts went running over and over in Ellen's head until she ached from the hounding of it. Hurts of the past and fears of the future kept playing ping-pong in the back of her brain. There was no peace with all this feverish mental activity. There was no place for God to love her or speak gently to her heart. Ellen was not present for this to happen. The "line was busy" with preoccupations. God could not reach her.

Story Three:

Jim is Ellen's husband. The same afternoon he dropped in to church on his way home from work. He, too, still carried the day's burdens on his back—the hassles at work, the mistakes in writing out orders, the snarls of traffic—all this and more. His "more" was like Ellen's more . . . the erosion of spontaneous warmth with his wife ("Whose fault is it?"); the inability to get the children to do their chores and quit quarrelling; the harmfulness of neighborhood gossip; the recent mistrust of an old friend; the sense of helplessness when his wife is depressed—not knowing what to say or do about it.

All this, and even more. Getting older. Passed up for a promotion. Money problems. The boss expects the impossible. There's not enough help. Too many on the job are inexcusably sloppy. "How can I do all the things I want to, for the home, church and community, when this job keeps bugging me!"

Then, besides the memory cranking out all these concerns, imagination starts to work on the mind, already soured. "Getting old?—You'll probably be fired soon!" "Money problems now?—You ain't seen nothin' yet!" "Hard times at work?—you never did reach the goals you set for yourself—worse failures are still to come!" "Your married life will probably get more dull and your children probably won't appreciate all you're trying to do for them!"

Whew! How dismal thoughts can escalate, even in the writing of them! One thought has a way of chasing another. And faster and faster the thoughts swirl the soul down into a whirlpool of indignation or rueful sadness.

Jim had wanted to pray. He meant well. But the time spent in church was worse than wasted. Just attempting to relax and to direct his heart to God pulled him off-guard from the normally high-geared momentum of his ordinary existence. He had no method of prayer—no way to screen off the noxious influences of hurts in the memory or anxieties in the imagination. He was not centered within himself. St. Peter warns us, "You must be self-controlled and alert to be able to pray." Jim was not. He was controlled by the demands of his boss, the displeasure of a friend, the uncooperativeness of workers and children, the despondency of his wife, the worries about the future of his family and himself. In the state he was in, if Jesus spoke to him (as He did so often to so many), "Do not be afraid—do not be anxious," Jim would probably have considered this advice no more helpful than telling an insomniac to "go to sleep and forget about it."

Jim, Ellen and Tom all need a method to prevent them from getting in that state. They need a way to harness memory and imagination so that they don't run wild, setting up bad vibrations in the mind and heart. They need to be present to the moment at hand, not pushed and pulled by the hurtful past or the dreaded future. They need guidance that will help them be more self-controlled (instead of controlled by people or past events). After self-control, they still need suggestions that will help them be alert to whatever God may want to communicate, however He may want to do so.

I went somewhat into detail with these three examples in order to put into relief the problem that faces all of us. Each one is different, of course. There are worries and hurts that come to different people in different ways—priests will have their own special variety; nuns theirs; nurses, farmers, lawyers, bakers, beggarmen, chiefs . . . like "occupational hazards," each has his/her "occupational hurts."

Different temperaments, also, will discover their own unique pattern of misunderstandings and dissatisfactions. Past mistakes and future worries have a different way of debilitating an extrovert or an introvert, an intuitive or an analytic thinker. Just the same, the problem still remains—how can we control distractions so that we can let prayer be what it is meant to be?

The method of "Guided Imagery" offers some assistance here. It sugests one way for a prayerful person to "de-obstaclize" those two formidable opponents to serenity. Guided imagery reasons that, "If you can't beat 'em, join 'em!"—or, rather, "let *them* join *you!*" Neither memory nor imagination can work both sides of the street at the same time. If they are already occupied in productive ways, they cannot get preoccupied in unproductive ones.

Memory can be of service as well as disservice. When left to its own devices, however, memory has a way of serving up bad news, as a rule. If Tom has 10 teachers and one of them gives him a bad time, that one will get the greatest exposure in his recollections. If Jim forgets one anniversary out of twenty-two, that one will loom large in his wife's ruminating brain and the other twenty-one will be cast off as inconsequential.

Memory cannot be left to its own devices. The will must dictate orders and stay in control. At least as much time should be given to good memories as to bad ones. Why do we let the hurts of the past arrogantly take control of all our "re-runs"? Republicans would be up in arms if the Democrats were able to control all the media during the election year; Democrats would likewise be aroused if the Republicans had such an unfair advantage. Yet, in our own brains—in that "little cinema" where the documentaries of the past are played again and again—this over-exposure of the bad side of our memory and under-exposure of our good side goes on and on.

Another way of putting it is this: Suppose you left for summer vacation and, on your return, you discovered that every light in the house was left on all that time. You would be furious with yourself—all that waste of electricity . . . used up . . . burned out . . . to no purpose.

But that foolish waste of kilowatt energy is nothing compared to what we do in the house that is called our brain:

1. when we keep alive the hurts and grudges of the past;
2. when we grumble about unpleasant people, futilely wishing some magic wand could be applied that would change them into pleasant people;
3. when we worry about the future with anxious "What ifs" ("What if this happens . . ." "What if they can't accept me . . ." "What if the market crashes and I can't send my boy to college . . ." "What if I slip on a banana peel and can't make the Junior Prom . . .")

Bitterness about the past can't change the past; fussing over unpleasantness can't get others to be more pleasant; anxiety about the future can't influence the stockmarket or make the banana skin go away. These are useless expenditures of energy, as wasteful as leaving the lights on when nobody's home. It is better, much better, to use our brain-energy when (and *only* when) it can do us some good.

The will can do something about the fixations of our memory. It can alert itself to the danger of fretfulness and re-direct the memory to successful achievements or pleasant associations.

Once the good side of our memory starts working, frayed nerves, caused by frustrations and mismanagements, are able to abate. The memory is soothed and the mind is free to be attentive to the present—to the possibilities of God working within us during the time of prayer.

Imagination, too, can help our meditation. Instead of teasing the mind with dire speculations of the future, imagination can begin the process of *hope*. We can give the imagination something to do in the *present* time. We can engage it in a mood of creative expectancy—"Perhaps Jesus will come and speak to me in the little room I just entered . . ." "Perhaps He will come and visit me in the meadow where I'm resting . . ."

When it is so engaged, imagination is too busy with the "plot" it is developing to be prophesying dooms or creating anxious thoughts. It is "busy with its playthings" so to speak. But it is not just playing. By getting the scene ready, it is helping the mind to be even more alert to whatever God may be pleased to evoke from our hearts. Imagination must not try to anticipate what Jesus will say. Imagination is meant to be simply the "stage manager" arranging the props and hoping the dialogue will turn out profitably. When this is accomplished, self-control and alertness will be achieved. God will do the rest . . . in whatever way He pleases.

Once memory and imagination are occupied in productive ways, they cannot harm us with their tendency to steer us off by their busy, nagging cogitations about past mistakes or future mishaps. They are productively at work:

in the service of the mind . . .
which is in the service of the present moment of prayer . . .
which is in the service of God.

Appendix 2

For those who wish to apply the reflections and meditations in this book to particular problems the material has been appropriately correlated and page numbers provided.

Appendix 3

For those desiring to use this book on a daily basis during Lent, the reflections and meditations have been correlated with the days of the season and page numbers provided.

Lenten Index

Photo credits: Pp. 10/11—So. African Tourist Corp.; p. 33—Swedish National Travel Office; pp. 51, 59, 81, 103—Jeff Brass; p. 55—Christopher Baldwin. All other photos from Twenty-Third Archives.